The Walter Lynwood Fleming
Lectures in Southern History
Louisiana State University

Place Over Time

Place
Over
Time

The Continuity of Southern Distinctiveness

CARL N. DEGLER

Louisiana State University Press

Baton Rouge and London

Copyright © 1977 by Louisiana State University Press
All rights reserved
Manufactured in the United States of America

Designer: Dwight Agner
Type face: VIP Melior
Typesetter: Graphic World, Inc., St. Louis, Missouri

Louisiana Paperback Edition, 1982

Author and publisher gratefully acknowledge permission to reprint
Chapter II, "The Beginnings of Southern Distinctiveness," which
originally appeared in *Southern Review*, XIII (Spring, 1977).

LIBRARY OF CONGRESS CATALOGING IN PUBLICATION DATA

Degler, Carl N
  Place over time.

  (The Walter Lynwood Fleming lectures in Southern history)
  Expanded versions of the author's lectures which were deliv-
ered at the Dept. of History, Louisiana State University, in 1976.
  Includes bibliographical references and index.
  1. Southern States—History. 2. Slavery in the United States.
3. Southern States—Social conditions. I. Title. II. Series.
F209.D43   975   77—586
ISBN 0-8071-0299-7 (cloth)
ISBN 0-8071-1031-0 (paper)

Were I inclined to continue this parallel, I could easily prove that almost all the differences which may be noticed between the characters of the Americans in the Southern and Northern states have originated in slavery.

      —Tocqueville

Contents

Preface and Acknowledgments   xi

I   The Distinctive South   1

II   The Beginnings of Southern
Distinctiveness   27

III   The Limited Distinctiveness of the
Old South   67

IV   The Persistence of Southern
Distinctiveness   99

Index   133

Preface and
Acknowledgments

THE IMMEDIATE origin of this little book was an invitation from the Department of History at Louisiana State University to deliver the Walter Lynwood Fleming Lectures in 1976. The deeper origins, however, are my long-held, twin interests in teaching and writing the history of the South. Although I was born and reared in New Jersey—northern New Jersey, to boot—I have been fascinated for almost as long as I can remember with the South. As someone once remarked to me, anyone born and reared in New Jersey, with its limited sense of identity and of place, might well develop a consuming interest in the South—where roots, place, family, and tradition are the essence of identity. Indeed, simply because I see that sense of locale and feeling persisting through the South's history I have called this book *Place Over Time*.

The subject of the book is that of the lectures I gave at Baton Rouge in April, 1976, but thanks to the gracious generosity of Louisiana State University Press, I have been able to expand the presentation in print. What appears here as Chapter III was not included in the lectures, because of the limitations of time in oral presentation. Yet from the beginning that material was an integral part of my overall subject, for the purpose behind the lectures as behind this book has been to deal with two large questions of southern history.

My first objective was to examine the connection between the South's present and its past. As I explain in more detail in the opening chapter, that connection has been a bone of contention among students of southern history. Some, like Wilbur J. Cash, maintain that the South's history runs in an essentially unbroken line from the antebellum days to the second half of the twentieth century. Others, like C. Vann Woodward, assert that the history of the region has been discontinuous, disrupted from time to time by such portentous happenings as emancipation, the Civil War, the Populist movement. My response to this contention runs throughout the four chapters and is distilled in the title.

My second goal was more complex. I have attempted to understand the nature of southern difference from the rest of the nation, yesterday and today. Recently it has become fashionable to argue that the South's admitted historic difference from the rest of the United States is now over, that the modern South has lost its distinctiveness. Contrary to that view, I conclude not only that the South is still distinctive but also that the origins of that distinctiveness can be traced back to the years of slavery and the plantation. It is the persistence into the second half of the twentieth century of the social and psychological characteristics that first appeared in the antebellum years which convinces me that southern history has indeed been continuous and without serious interruption.

In the course of developing this argument I perforce take issue with Eugene Genovese's interpretation of the antebellum South. Professor Genovese has contended that the profound impact of slavery upon the region made the antebellum South develop a world view radically different from that of the remainder of the United States. As I try to show, that interpretation seriously obscures the underlying similarity between antebellum southerners and other Americans, thus preventing us from recognizing the limits of southern distinctiveness.

Traditionally, southerners do not take easily to the dissection of their society and culture by outsiders, especially those who come from the North. Yet it is a measure of the South's self-criticism that many of the Fleming lecturers have been northerners. And certainly my own effort at analyzing what David Potter once called "the enigma of the South" was received with a critical attention that is the highest compliment that can be paid anyone's ideas. It is my pleasure here to thank the Department of History at Louisiana State University not only for providing me with the opportunity to put my ideas down on paper, but also for the cordial hospitality extended to my wife and me upon our visit there. Professor John Loos, chairman of the department, and Professor T. Harry Williams made sure that we saw, heard, and tasted—in the time at our disposal—what was memorable in Baton Rouge and its environs. The university, then in the midst of a delightfully balmy spring, provided a warm and attractive setting for our visit, which we shall recollect in tranquillity for years to come.

I wish also to thank Lewis Simpson, editor of the *Southern Review*, for publishing in his distinguished journal a portion of what appears here as Chapter II. My thanks go, too, to Jonathan Wiener, of the University of California at Irvine, and Barton Bernstein and Douglas Gamble, of Stanford University, who gave me the benefit of their critical readings of Chapter III; as a result, that chapter is sounder than it otherwise would have been. The anonymous reader of the manuscript for LSU Press has also earned my gratitude for his (or her) suggestions for improvements. I am also indebted to Beverly Jarrett, the managing editor of LSU Press, for her excellent, expeditious, and understanding editing of my prose; and readers ought to be, too. Of course, those weaknesses and errors that inevitably remain in these pages are to be charged against me alone.

Finally, it is only proper to acknowledge the help of literally dozens, perhaps hundreds of scholars in southern history whose researches I have relied upon for my evidence and ideas. Without that body of work this book could not be. In the interest of keeping the footnotes to a minimum I have not always identified the sources of my information with a full citation when a textual reference would serve that purpose. Since books referred to in the text by author can easily be located, I have not cited those in the footnotes except to provide my source for a direct quotation. As usual, I am also indebted to the Institute of American History at Stanford University for providing funds for typing costs.

C.N.D.

Place Over Time

I   The Distinctive South

AT ONE TIME in writing the series of lectures
from which this book derives, I entitled them "The Course of
the South to Distinctiveness," in remembrance of a famous
title of an essay by Ulrich B. Phillips. The resemblance between the two titles was certainly appropriate, for the distinctiveness of the South today, as in the past, is undoubtedly related to its having followed a course to secession. Indeed, that
act of withdrawal from the United States may well be taken as
the high point of southern distinctiveness. It was then that the
South, or at least a large portion of the region, sought to
realize itself as a separate national entity.

Even today, more than a century after that strike for independence, the South is a region set apart from the nation. Few
Americans deny its historical distinctiveness. Howard Zinn
in his book *Southern Mystique*, published over a decade ago,
stands out as one of those few who minimized differences between the South and the rest of the nation. His argument was
that those characteristics that are taken as southern, like racism, violence, nativism, and sexism, are simply American
characteristics writ larger. Few other observers, however,
have chosen to take Zinn's path. The more common argument
against the distinctiveness of the South has been one that actually admits it while denying it. I am thinking of those writ-

1

ers on the southern character who see the South being swallowed up in a rush to join the nation or being overwhelmed by modern technology and industrialization. John Egerton's *The Americanization of Dixie: The Southernization of America*, which appeared in 1974, sums up the point not only in the title, but also in the preface, where the author says "that for good and ill, the South is just about over as a separate and distinct place." [1] Over fifteen years earlier C. Vann Woodward made the same point with his metaphor of the "Bulldozer Revolution" in the South. By implication, of course, that approach assumes that until recently, at least, the South has been a distinctive region. Even when phrased in these qualified or historical terms, the denial of southern distinctiveness today is not entirely convincing. For not only was Woodward's observation made over fifteen years ago, only to be made again by Egerton, but almost twenty years ago, Harry Ashmore published *An Epitaph for Dixie*. In short, experience warns us that those who would bury the distinctive South, either by writing an epitaph or by saying *Farewell to the South*, as Robert Coles has recently done, may well find themselves in the position of those who prematurely announced the death of the most famous southern novelist.

The prevailing view today about the distinctiveness of the South was best expressed by V. O. Key, the distinguished analyst of modern southern politics who described the South in 1949 as "the region with the most distinctive character and tradition." [2] No, it is not the assertion that the South is distinctive within the nation that is at issue; rather it is the degree

1. John Egerton, *The Americanization of Dixie: The Southernization of America* (New York: Harper's Magazine Press, 1974), xxi.
2. V. O. Key, *Southern Politics in State and Nation* (New York: Alfred A. Knopf, 1949), ix.

and the persistence of that difference. The reason I dropped the title adapted from Phillips' essay is that I want to emphasize that my purpose in discussing distinctiveness is to demonstrate the essential continuity of southern history. Thus there are two questions to be examined: how distinctive is the South and to what extent was there continuity in the history of the region? Historians have divided on both questions. Let me begin to examine the question of the degree of southern distinctiveness, and after that we can turn to the issue of continuity, which, as we shall see, is closely related to the question of distinctiveness.

In the writings of southern historian Francis B. Simkins there is no doubt that the South was different from the rest of the nation, both in the past and in the present. His *The Everlasting South* proclaimed the idea in its title and in its text. Although many modern writers have contended in recent years, Simkins complained, that the South had long ceased to be different, the facts are quite otherwise. "There is no reason," he wrote in 1963, "to discard Stark Young's contention that 'the changing South is still the South'. Indeed, it can be argued that the region, despite many changes, is as much different from the rest of the United States today as it was in 1860."[3]

Simkins' conception of the distinctiveness of the South is considerably more pronounced than that of other historians. David M. Potter, for example, would not "deny that there was distinctiveness in the Southern culture," but he could not see that culture as so distinctive as to account for an historical event like the coming of the Civil War. "Southern conservativism, Southern hierarchy, the cult of chivalry, the un-

3. Francis B. Simkins, *The Everlasting South* (Baton Rouge: Louisiana State University Press, 1963), xii.

machined civilization, the folk society, the rural character of the life, the clan values rather than the commercial values— all had a deep significant distinctiveness," he admitted. Yet "this is not quite the same as *separateness*, and the efforts of historians to buttress their claim that the South had a wholly separate culture, self-consciously asserting itself as a cultural counterpart of political nationalism, have led, on the whole, to paltry results," he concluded.[4]

Still other historians have gone even farther in minimizing the differences between North and South. Charles Grier Sellers, Jr., in *The Southerner as American* and Grady McWhiney in *Southerners and Other Americans* stress the similarities in southern and American cultures. McWhiney, for example, concludes that "the evidence indicates that differences between races and sections were no more pronounced than similarities." Indeed, he calls the idea "that when the Civil War began Southerners were fundamentally different from Northerners . . . one of the great myths of American history. . . . Writers, intent upon showing the Civil War era's conflicts and controversies, have tended to magnify the differences between Northerners and Southerners out of all proportion," he argued. "In 1861 the United States did not contain, as some people have suggested, two civilizations."[5]

All of the historians who minimize the differences freely admit a divergence between the South and the non-South on an issue like slavery. But they tend to see slavery as an anomaly, a burden that southern whites struggled under, if not always against. Sellers, for instance, calls his own chapter in

4. David M. Potter, *The South and the Sectional Conflict* (Baton Rouge: Louisiana State University Press, 1968), 68–69.
5. Grady McWhiney, *Southerners and Other Americans* (New York: Basic Books, Inc., 1973), 3–4.

The Southerner as American "The Travail of Slavery." His argument is that southerners were deeply ambivalent, even guilt-ridden about slavery simply because they were Americans, too. Even Kenneth M. Stampp, the historian of slavery, has set forth a version of this view in an essay entitled "The Southern Road to Appomattox," the substance of which is that the South breathed a collective sigh of relief when slavery was ended by northern fiat.[6] To Stampp, slavery was a burden the South took on early in its history and was even prepared to fight to preserve, but it was far from unhappy that the institution disappeared in the holocaust of war. An implication that can be drawn from his essay is that the cultural differences between South and North were limited before the war and were, thus, considerably reduced thereafter.

Quite the opposite emphasis is seen in the work of Eugene Genovese, who considers the culture of the antebellum South so different from the North's that he talks of a divergence in world views or in fundamental values. C. Vann Woodward, too, has advanced this conception of the differences between North and South before the Civil War. His summation of the nature of the antebellum South depicts it as a "great slave society, by far the largest and richest of those that had existed in the New World since the sixteenth century, [which] had grown up and miraculously flourished in the heart of a thoroughly bourgeois and partly puritanical republic. It had renounced its bourgeois origins and elaborated and painfully rationalized its institutional, legal, metaphysical, and religious defenses. It had produced leaders of skill, ingenuity, and strength who, unlike those of other slave societies, invested their honor and their lives, and not merely part of their

---

6. Kenneth M. Stampp, "The Southern Road to Appomattox," *Cotton Memorial Papers*, No. 4 (February, 1969), University of Texas at El Paso.

capital, in that society. When the crisis came, they, unlike the others, chose to fight. It proved to be the death struggle of a society, which went down in ruins."[7]

Genovese, unlike Woodward, has not written about the years after the Civil War, but it is clear from his and from Woodward's conception of the society of the antebellum South that to them the war was a discontinuity in the history of the South. Indeed, Woodward has been quite explicit in setting forth his belief that the discontinuity in southern history is in marked contrast with the continuity of American history in general. It is discontinuity, Woodward contends, that "helps to account for the distinctiveness of the South and its history."[8] More recently he described the South as "long unique among the regions of the nation for abrupt and drastic breaks in the continuity of its history."[9] Southern historian Paul Gaston has also emphasized the sharp line between the Old South and the New. He accuses W. J. Cash of "misjudging the significance of key elements in the Southern experience; the Old-New South dichotomy which he minimizes is in fact a crucial one with which every search for the 'central theme' of Southern history must come to terms at one point or another."[10] It is true that W. J. Cash minimizes the discontinuities. In his evocative book *The Mind of the South* he makes quite explicit his conception of the southern past. "The extent of the change and the break between the Old South that was and the South of our time has been vastly exaggerated," he writes. "The South, one might say, is a tree with many age

---

7. C. Vann Woodward, *American Counterpoint: Slavery and Racism in the North-South Dialogue* (Boston: Little, Brown & Company, 1971), 281.

8. *Ibid.*, 275.

9. C. Vann Woodward, *Origins of the New South* (Rev. ed.; Baton Rouge: Louisiana State University Press, 1971), vii.

10. Paul M. Gaston, *The New South Creed: A Study in Southern Mythmaking* (New York: Alfred A. Knopf, 1970), 11–12.

rings, with its limbs and trunks bent and twisted by all the winds of the years, but with its tap root in the Old South." [11]

My intention in this book is to demonstrate the continuity in southern history that has been either explicitly or implicitly denied by recent historians of the South like Woodward, Genovese, and Gaston. I propose to demonstrate that the modern distinctiveness of the South has its origins in the remote past, my assumption being that a South which is distinctive in the same ways over an extended period of time is a South whose history is without serious discontinuities. I recognize that in doing this I run the danger of constructing a monolithic South, a region without internal differences, a people without diversity—a South, in sum, that never was. But since I have elsewhere written at book-length about *The Other South*, I believe I can be excused if here I dwell upon the undoubted reality of *The* South. Let it simply be understood in the pages that follow that underneath and behind all of the generalizations and assertions of southern identity, the diversity that is also a part of the South is taken for granted, not ignored or denied.

To establish the continuity of the South's history we must first look at the nature of southern distinctiveness today; then we can turn to exploring the roots. There is, of course, a large literature on southern identity, but I will neither resurrect nor dissect it here. The fact of the South's identity is not as difficult as the worried literature on the subject makes out. Obviously, what the South is has both subjective and objective components. I intend to deal with both, but principally with the objective aspects that mark the South as a distinctive region. My approach to the question of southern identity is simple. Central to my definition of the South is that if there is

11. W. J. Cash, *The Mind of the South* (New York: Alfred A. Knopf, 1941), x.

a South then the people who live there should recognize their kinship with one another and, by the same token, those who live outside the South ought to recognize that southerners are somehow different from them. That is the subjective part of the approach I will follow. The objective part is that if there is in fact a South that exists outside the subjective images in the heads of Americans, it ought to be objectively discernible.

Let me look first, and briefly, at the subjective and self-conscious identification of the South. In 1957 the Gallup Poll asked a number of people spread across some forty states three questions: "Do you like Southern food"; "Do you like the Southern accent"; and "Do you like Southern girls?" The highest possible score was three, that is, a "yes" answer to all three questions. Those surveyed states that are generally denominated southern—the eleven states of the former Confederacy plus Kentucky and Maryland—had a mean score of 2.03. (Over 70 percent of the people queried answered "yes" to two or three of the questions.) The nonsouthern states' mean score was 1.03. (Only 29 percent answered two or three questions affirmatively.) In fact, no state outside those thirteen reached a score as high as 1.5; and only Washington, Arizona, New Mexico, West Virginia, and Missouri scored as high as 1.3.[12] And both West Virginia and Missouri had at one time been slave states.

This preference test does more than simply identify the states of the South. It suggests that there is not only a South, but a South that is subjectively recognized by insiders and outsiders alike. One of the identifying elements of a minority or ethnic group is a sense of difference from others that is internalized, as well as evident in comparisons with those

12. John Shelton Reed, *The Enduring South: Subcultural Persistence in Mass Society* (Lexington, Mass.: D. C. Heath, 1972), 10–26 discusses the various measures of southern identity referred to on this page and the next.

outside the group. John Shelton Reed, a young southern sociologist, has recently tried to measure the strength of that sense of group cohesion or identification. When he asked a number of people whether they had an interest in, or sympathy for, a series of different social groups, he found that white southerners had higher indices of identification with their region than labor union members or Roman Catholics had with their organizations. (White southerners, on the other hand, had less sense of identification than did black southerners or Jews.) Even more striking is the finding of another attitudinal survey reported by Reed—that southerners and northerners viewed themselves as less alike than male and female persons, rural and urban people, and immigrants and natives. In the light of this sense of difference, it is not strange that Lewis Killian, in his book *White Southerners*, treats southerners as an ethnic group. Something of the source of that sense of difference, as well a measure of it, is revealed in a personal anecdote Killian told his editor. When Georgia-born Killian first went to the University of Massachusetts to teach, the editor writes, "he moved through a reception line of new faculty. Ahead of him were several Europeans. Despite thick accents, they were greeted without comment. When he got to the head of the line and introduced himself [in his Georgia drawl], he was asked if he longed for home. At that point, he reports, he did." [13]

Surveys of attitudes and personal testimony do not tell us much about the content or sources of this sense of difference or about the reasons for group cohesion. Another survey by John Shelton Reed of forty-seven white southern college students in 1970, however, offers a clue to both the nature and the origins. The students were asked to list adjectives that de-

13. Lewis Killian, *White Southerners* (New York: Random House, 1970), x.

scribe northerners, southerners, and Americans. The four
most popular descriptions of white southerners were *conservative, tradition-loving, courteous,* and *loyal to family ties.*
White northerners were depicted in the same order of popu-
larity as *industrious, materialistic* and *intelligent* (tied for
second place), *progressive,* and *sophisticated.* Significantly,
the adjectives most often selected to describe Americans in
general came very close to the top four used to identify northerners, though the forty-seven students making the listings
were all white southerners. Americans in general were described as *materialistic, intelligent* and *industrious* (tied for
second place), *pleasure-loving,* and *progressive.* Clearly, these
southern students were identifying the North with America
and seeing themselves as deviating in a traditional or conservative direction from other Americans.

Having examined a few of the subjective measures of
southern identity, let us consider some of the more objective
characteristics that seem to set off the society of the modern
South from the remainder of the United States. Probably the
most apparent and least disputed objective difference between the South and the rest of the nation is that the South is
the region with the hottest weather. Arizona and Nevada may
have average yearly temperatures that are higher, but they
lack the humidity that makes the South's summers uniquely
oppressive and its springs delightfully balmy. The South, in
short, is the only section of the country that comes close to a
tropical climate—and some parts of it come very close.

Some commentators of southern distinctiveness have been
bold enough to attribute human behavior to the influence of
climate. Rupert Vance, for example, described southerners as
not coming in out of the rain because the weather is so mild;
somewhat more seriously, he maintained that in the past
southerners had failed to construct sound, tight barns because

they lacked the stimulus of the harsh winters of New England or the Middle West. Hookworm, Vance goes on, was endemic to the South because the mild climate encouraged people to go without shoes and thus lay themselves open to infection through the feet. James Dabbs correlated the violence of southern summer thunderstorms with the violence of the people, arguing that the weather was an irritation, goading southerners to acts of passion and violence. Clarence Cason shaped his *Ninety Degrees in the Shade* around the weather as an explanation for the southerner's slowness of speech and action. And certainly to a northerner, even in the age of airconditioning, the South's summer heat and humidity are obvious, if not sufficient, explanations for the slower pace of life in Dixie. Moreover, the architecture of the colonial and antebellum South, not to say the positioning of the great houses along the Battery in Charleston, testifies to the impact of hot summers and mild winters.

It is not my purpose here, however, to offer the climate as explanation for the social or psychological distinctiveness of the South; I want merely to note that the climate indubitably sets the South apart from the remainder of the nation. One way it does so is by providing a unique arena in which history was played out. In that respect, least, the climate has had a passive, if not active, influence in shaping the region's past. Certainly the South's historic commitment to agriculture can be traced in large part to its climate. The climate did not *make* men grow tobacco or cotton, but the climate did make it possible for them to grow those crops that had set the South's agriculture apart from that of the North. Cotton requires a growing season of two hundred frost-free days, a longer period than the climate of any other region of the nation can duplicate except the Southwest and California. And even in those much more recently settled places, the lack of adequate rainfall has allowed competition with the South only in this century. Tobacco of sorts can be grown in the North, but the best tobacco is still grown in the South; and, of course, rice and sugar, like cotton, are wholly confined to the region of long growing seasons free from frost.

That the climate permitted the growth of these peculiarly southern crops goes a long way to explaining why the South is the only region of the United States that developed plantation agriculture. Certainly the plantation did not spread in the South because of the climate; but without a climate favorable to tobacco, cotton, sugar, and rice southern agriculture would probably have been like that of the North in both crops and organization. The great staples encouraged the use of dependent labor to meet the world demand, thus creating the plantation. Today Mississippi is only the third instead of the first producer of cotton, as it was for so long, yet the South remains the land of cotton as it has been for almost two centuries.

Recently, Julius Rubin has suggested that climate has had a more active role in differentiating southern agriculture from that of the rest of the nation.[14] Acknowledging that none of the South lies in the tropics, he observes that the climate of much of the South nonetheless approximates tropical conditions. The lack of deep and prolonged frosts permits the survival of parasites that reduce livestock size and production; frequent heavy rains leach the soil of nutrients and reduce crop yields unless fertilizers are used. Heavy rains also produce acid soils that limit crop selection and yields, while the long, hot summers make the growing of shallow-root crops difficult. Fodder crops in particular were hard to grow in the South, thus limiting the combination of food crops and livestock that encouraged the profitable small-farmer agriculture

14. Julius Rubin, "Limits of Agricultural Progress in the Nineteenth Century South," *Agricultural History*, XLIX (April, 1975), 362–73.

of the North. Rather than seeing southern agricultural success as a function of its climate and soil, Rubin persuasively argues that what success the South achieved in agriculture in the antebellum years should be attributed to economic factors outside the South—like the strong world demand for cotton, which overcame rather noticeable handicaps from the southern climate.

Although the South has several characteristics of a tropical climate, it actually exists entirely outside the tropical zone. That fact offers another measure of its distinctiveness. For if within the United States the South is distinctive as the only plantation society, among the plantation societies of the New World it is the only one located entirely outside the tropics. One social consequence of this is that the South was the only slave society in which whites outnumbered blacks. For a variety of reasons, not least of which were the tropical heat and diseases, all the other plantation societies of the New World failed to attract many white settlers and even fewer white women. White Americans lacked the encouragement toward intermarriage or interbreeding that was present in the other plantation societies and that often did much to soften relations between the races. Thus, on two counts relating to its plantation system, the South stands out as historically different, if not unique.

But the history of the South's differences is not my prime concern right now. Rather, my aim is to isolate those aspects of the modern South that distinguish it from other regions of the United States. For my intention is to show the continuity of southern history by demonstrating that the distinctive elements of the modern South originated early in the region's history and that they have persisted all through that history.

Today, as a century ago, the South is the most agricultural region of the country. As recently as 1940, the census counted

40 percent of white southerners as rural farm residents, whereas only 16 percent of the white people living outside the South were thus described. And even as late as 1960, some 11 percent of the whites and 14 percent of the blacks in the South were still designated as rural farm people, as contrasted with 6.4 percent whites and 1.2 percent blacks in the non-South.

The other side of the coin in the South's continuing emphasis upon agriculture is the small number of cities in the region as compared to the rest of the United States. It is true, as C. Vann Woodward and others have pointed out, that the *rate* of urbanization in the South today is higher than in any region of the country. But in every southern state the proportion of the population living in cities is still smaller than the national average. Half of the people of the South today live in metropolitan regions, but the national average is two-thirds. Even in the upper or border South, city people are in the minority in some states. Most North Carolinians and West Virginians, for example, do *not* live in any urban place of twenty-five hundred people or more; and according to the census of 1970, only a bare majority of Kentuckians and Tennesseans live in cities that large. Even the big cities of the South are noticeably smaller than those of other sections of the country. There are six cities of one million or more population in the United States, but only one—Houston—is in the South. Put another way, according to the 1970 census, 80 percent of all urban Southerners live in cities between fifty thousand and one million population, while 60 percent of the urban population of the north-central states (the Middle West) and 75 percent of that of the northeastern states live in cities of one million.

This ancient and persistent rurality of the South has been cited by some observers as a principal reason for the South's remarkable literary achievement, especially in the twentieth century. Malcolm Cowley, for instance, has traced the roots of William Faulkner's genius, Truman Capote's family tales, Eudora Welty's gems of local portraiture, Thomas Wolfe's prodigality of words, Ellen Glasgow's insightful social commentary, Tennessee Williams' explorations of love and violence, and the works of half a dozen other well-known southern writers to the rural dweller's propensity to talk and spin stories. As Eudora Welty herself has said:

Southerners . . . love a good tale. They are born reciters, great memory retainers, diary keepers, letter exchangers, and letter savers, history tracers, and debaters, and—outstaying all the rest—great talkers. Southern talk is on the narrative side, employing the verbatim conversation. For this, plenty of time is needed and it is granted. It was still true not so very far back that children grew up listening— listening through unhurried stretches of uninhibited reminiscence, and listening galvanized. They were naturally prone to be entertained from the first by life as they heard tell of it, and to feel free, encouraged, and then in no time compelled, to pass their pleasure on.[15]

Plausible as the relationship suggested here between rurality and the South's undoubted achievement in literature may be, it probably will not stand much scrutiny. After all, the region has been rural for a long time; yet its literacy achievement is chiefly a twentieth-century phenomenon. Even if rurality cannot be accepted as an explanation for the southern literary renaissance, it still deserves recognition as a characteristic that sets the region apart. And there are other distinguishing characteristics of the South that can be traced with more confidence to its rurality.

That the South is the most rural and least urbanized region

15. Quoted in Neal R. Peirce, *The Deep South States of America: People, Politics, and Power in the Seven Deep South States* (New York: W. W. Norton, 1974), 44.

of the country is surely related to the fact that today it is also the poorest. Only those states of the South on the periphery of the region—Texas, Virginia, and Florida—come close to the national figures of per-capita income. Even so, in the 1970 census, Virginia and Florida fell below the national average. All the states of the upper South, which are heavily white in racial composition, reported higher proportions of their populations below the poverty line in 1970 than the nation at large. Slightly less than 11 percent of Americans in 1970 were counted as below the poverty level; the six states of the upper South ranged from 12.3 percent in Virginia to 19.2 percent in Kentucky. I cite the figures for the upper or border South because it is commonly thought that these states are better off than is the Deep South, with its greater proportion of blacks and its historic emphasis upon one-crop agriculture. And to a certain extent that assumption is true; yet the upper southern states, like the region as a whole, are still poorer than any states outside the South. In 1969 no state of the former Confederacy counted less than 20 percent of its population below the poverty line, and four of them plus Kentucky reported proportions above 30 percent. As the New York *Times* reported on August 17, 1975, two out of every three impoverished Americans living in nonmetropolitan areas were southerners. And these figures were collected after a decade in which the states of the Deep South showed a faster growth in per-capita income than the nation as a whole. No state of the Deep South equaled the per-capita income of the nation in 1969; even Texas and Florida fell below. Ironically enough, it was the outflow of poor black people during the 1960s that made the decade's improvement as great as it was.

The rurality of the South is only a part of the reason for its poverty. I am not trying to explain the poverty of the South by reference to its rurality, for that is only an element in the explanation. Yet it is true that in most developed countries today the principal sources of increasing wealth or economic growth are related to gains in manufacturing. Certainly, the South's own improvement in its per-capita income over the past thirty years is related to the increasing proportion of its population engaged in manufacturing. Yet here, too, the South is set apart from the nation. The average hourly wage for workers in industry in the South continues to lag behind that of the nation. In 1963, for example, workers in not a single one of the eleven former Condederate states received average hourly wages equal to those received by manufacturing workers in other sections of the country. There are, of course, a number of explanations for this discrepancy, not the least important of which is that the South's manufactures happen to be low-wage industries. But whatever the explanation, the fact of difference remains, just as another difference persists. The South has a smaller proportion of its nonagricultural workers unionized than does the nation in general. In 1966 the proportion of unionized workers did not reach 20 percent in any of the states of the former Confederacy, and in some the proportion was considerably lower. The figure for the nation at that time was almost 29 percent. Moreover, the South has led the nation in enacting laws to counter labor unions. As George Mowry pointed out, "At the end of the 1950s every Southern state except Kentucky had some variety of right to work law upon its statute books." [16]

The rurality of the South and the paucity of cities together foster another characteristic that sets the South apart from the nation at large. Demographically the South is distinguished today, as in the past, by the homogeneity of its European stock and the duality of its racial makeup. Today, the South con

16. George Mowry, *Another Look at the Twentieth-Century South* (Baton Rouge: Louisiana State University Press, 1973), 79.

tains proportionately more blacks than any other section of the country, though some states of the South now have fewer blacks than some northern states. And that is true even though in the last sixty years the proportion of American blacks who live in the South has dropped from 90 percent to slightly more than 50 percent. Despite the great northward Negro migration of the twentieth century, the South is still the region where most blacks live and where a larger porportion of the population is Negro.

It is, of course, this concentration of black people in the South that has often been cited to explain certain southern racial attitudes. Ulrich B. Phillips, for example, located the central theme of southern history in the determination that the South was and would remain a white man's country. The sources of southern white attitudes toward blacks are obviously diverse, but they are certainly related to the demographic fact that the South's population has always contained a higher proportion of Negroes than the rest of the United States. This fact has differentiated the South not only in the minds of southerners, but in the minds of other Americans as well.

If the South has been diverse in race, it has been just the opposite in ethnicity. During the nineteenth and twentieth centuries, when the United States as a whole received some forty million immigrants, the South's share was disproportionately small. All through its history the South's white population has derived overwhelmingly from northwestern Europe. At the same time, the rest of the country's population has been broadly diversified with Chinese and Japanese from Asia, Italians, Poles, Russians, and Greeks from southern and eastern Europe, and Irish, Germans, and English from northwestern Europe. Actually, even to speak of the South as peopled by northwestern Europeans overstates the case since few Norwegians, Swedes, or Danes came to the South, though several states in the Middle West and Great Plains were heavily populated by these nationalities.

This lack of diversified immigration into the South has also narrowed the region's range of religions, thus further setting it apart from the rest of the nation. Today, as Will Herberg has pointed out, the United States is religiously tripartite; it cannot any longer be perceived, as it was in the nineteenth century, as a Protestant country. Rather it must be seen as Protestant, Catholic, and Jewish. The Catholic and Jewish components, of course, are the result of massive immigration from southern Ireland, Germany, Italy, Poland, and Russia in the late nineteenth and early twentieth centuries. Today, as a result, the South is the most Protestant region of the country. Indeed, if one looks at a religious atlas of the United States, one cannot help being struck by the almost total absence of Catholic counties in the southern states. The principal exceptions are along the Mexican border in Texas and in southern Louisiana. With the single exception of Utah and its heavy concentration of Mormons, only states in the South are without at least one Roman Catholic county. The Jews are too few to show up on a religious atlas, except in New York City, but it is perhaps enough to note that Harry Golden and his *North Carolina Israelite* were notable as much for the paucity of their duplicates in the South as for their wit and wisdom.

What relative absence of Jews, Catholics, Poles, Chinese, Italians, and Greeks might mean in the making of southern identity has been well suggested by the southern writer Willie Morris. Born and reared in Yazoo City, Mississippi, Morris went to the University of Texas and in time to New York City and the editorship of *Harper's Magazine*. In his autobiography *North Toward Home*, Morris tells how impressed he was when reading books "like Alfred Kazin's haunting poetic

reminiscences of boyhood in an immigrant Jewish neighbor-
hood in the East." Morris could only marvel at the "vast gulf
that separates that kind of growing up and the childhood and
adolescence of those of us who came out of the towns of the
American South and Southwest a generation later. With the
Eastern Jewish intellectuals, who play such a substantial part
in American cultural life, perhaps in the late 1960s, a dominant part," he writes, "the struggle as they grew up in the
1930s was for one set of ideas over others, for a fierce acceptance or rejection of one man's theories or another man's
poetry—and with all this a driving determination to master
the language which had not been their parents' and to find a
place in a culture not quite theirs." How different, he goes on,
that environment was from the one that young southerners
grew up in, or even experienced at the university.

Where an Alfred Kazin at the age of nineteen might become aroused
in the subway by reading a review by John Chamberlain in the *New
York Times* and rush to his office to complain, we at eighteen or
nineteen were only barely beginning to learn that there *were* ideas,
much less ideas to arouse one from one's self. If places like City College or Columbia galvanized the young New York intellectuals already drenched in literature and polemics, the University of Texas
had, in its halting, unsure, and often frivolous way, to teach those of
us with good minds and small town high school diplomas that we
were intelligent human beings with minds and hearts of our own
that we might learn to call our own, that there were some things,
many things—ideas, values, choices of action—worth committing
one's self to and fighting for, that a man in some instances might become morally committed to honoring every manifestation of individual conscience and courage.[17]

Less subtle social behavior is also explicable by reference
to the South's lack of religious and ethnic diversity. It is
surely difficult for a Ku Klux Klan that opposes immigrants,

17. Willie Morris, *North Toward Home* (Boston: Houghton, Mifflin,
1967), 149–50.

as the Klan of the 1920s predominantly did, to thrive in states where immigrants make up a substantial and often a politically powerful part of the population. In states like Indiana and Oregon, where the proportion of the native-born was almost as high as it was in the South, the Klan in the 1920s was both active and strong. Lack of familiarity with Jews undoubtedly has a good deal to do with the greater hesitancy among southerners, according to opinion polls, in voting for a Jewish candidate for president. In 1959 a national survey asked citizens whether they would vote for a candidate of their party who was Jewish. A third of southern voters answered negatively, as compared with 11 percent of voters in the Northeast, 22 percent in the West, and 25 percent in the Middle West.[18]

The South's paucity of immigration has helped to shape its attitudes toward the world. Samuel Lubell some time ago argued that American isolationism toward Europe in the 1930s, centered as it was in the Middle West, was a function of the immigrant composition of that region. The large number of people of German and Scandinavian descent in the Middle West was the basis of the region's opposition to involvement in the European war of 1939. If that explanation is valid, then the South's small proportion of immigrants might well account for the well-known weakness of isolationist sentiment in the region during the 1930s. By the same token, the South's reputation as the most nationalistic section of the country is surely related to the fact that its perception of the rest of the world is the least clouded—or, if one prefers, the least sensitized by the presence of this or that ethnic or national group of citizens with a continuing stake in European, Middle Eastern, or Asian affairs.

18. Alfred O. Hero, Jr., "Southern Jews," in L. Dinnerstein and M. D. Palsson (eds.), *Jews in the South* (Baton Rouge: Louisiana State University Press, 1973), 241.

I leave aside at this point, as I have in regard to the rurality and poverty of the South, the reasons for these demographic differences. Accounting for them is the job of subsequent chapters. Suffice to say here that all of these aspects of southern difference—the emphasis upon agriculture, the poverty, the dearth of cities, and the paucity of immigrants—are interrelated in origins and dialectic in social effects.

The small number of Catholics and Jews in the South is not the only religion-related condition that helps to set the South apart from the rest of the country. Both systematic public-opinion polls and impressionistic evidence concur in concluding that the South is the most religious region of the country and, further, that the character of its Protestantism is traditional and conservative. In a 1966 poll, for example, 86 percent of southerners who identified themselves as Protestants said they believed in the Devil; in the same survey only 52 percent of Protestants and 65 percent of Catholics in the rest of the country so believed. Moreover, a much larger proportion of southern Protestants believed in the Second Coming of Christ than Protestants or Catholics in the non-South. Even when these responses are standardized for differences in educational background and degree of urbanization, southerners still come out as much as 30 percentage points higher than other Protestants in regard to belief in the existence of the Devil and some 17 percentage points higher than northern Protestants in acceptance of a literal interpretation of the New Testament.[19]

The conservatism of southern religious attitudes can be further measured by the lack of peripheral religious sects in the South. There are few Mormons or Christian Scientists in the region, and because of the small number of immigrants,

19. Reed, *The Enduring South*, 60–81, contains these opinion poll results.

few Lutherans. Moreover, the "Social Gospel," which caused many Protestant churches in the North to become concerned with problems of the working class, with urbanites, and with international affairs in the early twentieth century, scarcely touched the South. Its dominant Baptist and Methodist churches remained strongly individualistic and evangelical.

Religion helps to set the South apart from the nation not only because it is conservative, but also because it is taken seriously by southerners. The southern commitment to conservative religion has often been deplored by a secular nation. And it is true that the strong religious beliefs of southerners were among the prime sources for the illiberal antievolution laws that were passed in a number of southern states in the 1920s. But it is often forgotten that it was the equally serious religious commitment of liberal southern religious leaders like William Louis Poteat of Wake Forest College that prevented such laws from being enacted in North Carolina and Kentucky. For a more recent example of the liberal social consequences of a southerner's religious convictions one need only read former Arkansas Congressman Brooks Hays's book *A Southern Moderate Speaks*. As Hays tells the story, it was his Christian belief in the equality of blacks and whites before God and the law that moved him to take a stand in favor of integration in the Little Rock crisis of 1957, a public commitment that resulted in the loss of his congressional seat. An even more recent example would be the connection between the strong religious convictions of Reuben Askew or Jimmy Carter and their public positions on racial equality.

Actually, the South's conservatism in religion is part of a broader conservative outlook among southerners, despite the effort of some liberal southern historians to minimize it. Public-opinion polls reveal this conservatism quite clearly. During the 1950s, for example, sociologist Samuel Stoffer compared the conservatism of southerners with that of other Americans by measuring their respective toleration of Socialists, atheists, and those whose national loyalty was then being questioned. Deliberately, he avoided the race question. Westerners turned out to be the most tolerant, with over two-fifths saying they would accept all of these deviant groups; but only 14 percent of southerners in one poll and 18 percent on another would tolerate them. Middle westerners were almost twice as tolerant as southerners. And even when the scores were broken down into degrees of rurality on the assumption that the South's conservatism might simply be a function of its relative lack of urbanization, southerners still came out as considerably less tolerant than the residents of the other three regions. A more recent measure of southern conservatism in politics is the report by the *Congressional Quarterly* in 1971 that "for the second year in a row, Southern senators and representatives supported Nixon more than their colleagues from any other part of the country. The Southern support cut across party lines."[20]

Another way in which the South is differentiated from the rest of the nation is in its tendency toward personal violence. Southern observers, like Charles Sydnor, John Hope Franklin, Sheldon Hackney, and John Shelton Reed, have been among those emphasizing this characteristic of southern society.[21] The earliest full study of southern violence in a comparative perspective showed that the homicide rate per 100,000 persons in the South in 1920–1924 was about 2.5 times as great as that for the remainder of the country. Twice since then, ac-

20. Quoted in Egerton, *The Americanization of Dixie*, 6.
21. Charles S. Sydnor, "The Southerner and the Laws," *Journal of Southern History*, VI (February, 1940), 3–24; John Hope Franklin, *The Militant South, 1800–1861* (Cambridge, Mass.: Harvard University Press, 1956); Sheldon Hackney, "Southern Violence," *American Historical Review*, LXXIV (February, 1969), 906–25; John Shelton Reed, "To Live—And Die—in Dixie: A Contribution to the Study of Southern Violence," *Political Science Quarterly*, LXXXVI (September, 1971), 429–43.

cording to Sheldon Hackney, similar comparative studies have turned up similar results. That we need to talk about personal violence and not simply crime is shown by the fact that in 1973, all the states of the former Confederacy, with the exceptions of Virginia and Arkansas, exceeded the national rate for murders, whereas among those same eleven states only Florida exceeded the national rate for robbery. In 1968 over half of southern white families owned guns as compared to slightly more than a quarter of the families in the non-South. When a federal gun control law passed Congress in 1968, by a vote of 304 to 118, the representatives from the former Confederate states voted against it 73 to 19.

On the other hand, it is significant that the suicide rate in the South, as Sheldon Hackney has pointed out, is below the national average. Hackney suggests that this connects the personal violence in the South with the region's sense of being a minority, of being put upon, since the violence is clearly not directed against the self, but against others. Southerners also score much lower in regard to crimes against property than do people in other sections of the country. So it is not crime as such that sets southerners apart from other Americans, but personal violence directed against others. If that violence is a consequence of a southern sense of frustration, of being a minority, then that characteristic of the South, like the others we have looked at, is best explained by reference to the history of the region. Indeed, it is my contention that not only can these distinguishing characteristics be accounted for through the history of the South, but that the persistence of them throughout a long stretch of that history is evidence of the underlying continuity of southern history. I will now try to set forth some of those historical circumstances that have shaped the modern South and thereby given a striking continuity to its history.

II   The Beginnings
of Southern Distinctiveness

IF ONE contemplates the various measures of the South's difference from the rest of the nation today, a rather obvious historical explanation comes to mind. Characteristics like the prominence of blacks, the rurality of the region, the dependence upon agriculture, and the persistence of violence are all consistent with the presence of plantation slavery. Certainly, the South has long been known as the one region of the country in which the plantation *and* slavery went together. Other regions may have had slavery, but no other region developed and maintained the plantation. But if plantation slavery is taken as a central explanation for the evolution of a different South, then the origins of the South must be pushed back to the earliest years of the nation. The plantation, after all, began in the South in the seventeenth century and was resting securely upon the labor of black slaves by the opening years of the eighteenth century. Long before the Revolution, in short, the South was a land of plantations and slaves. But was there such a thing as "the South" that early in American history?

The researches of John Blassingame certainly give us pause in pushing back so far into the eighteenth century the identification of the South. His examination of the writing of contemporaries at the time of the Revolution shows that there

27

may have been a strong sense of identification with locality or even with provinces, but he found no references to "the South" or "Southern provinces" as we would apply those terms today. When such phrases were used they could include any province south of New York—hardly a usage that fits our conception of the plantation South today. Never, Blassingame writes, did the colonists who lived south of the Mason-Dixon Line refer to themselves as southerners. Blassingame would apparently accept Patrick Henry's categories when that colonial proclaimed himself not a Virginian, but an American.[1]

Some other evidence, however, after the Revolution had been fought and won, suggests that a sense of regionalism might well have been present during, perhaps even before, the Revolution, despite Blassingame's findings, though it was submerged by the immediate need to identify with other Americans in the course of the crisis with Britain. Certainly, Virginia Loyalist Jonathan Boucher, even before the Revolution broke out, made an appeal to other southerners in Congress to avoid rupture with Britain on the grounds that the southern colonies were vulnerable in ways that northerners were not. That he was talking about the slave South is evident from his remark that "exceedingly different from the northern colonies, we have within ourselves an enemy fully equal to all our strength," alluding to the fact that though all the northern states had slaves, they constituted only a small fraction of the population of those states. In his book *The First South*, John Alden has advanced an array of evidence to suggest that southerners perceived themselves as different from norther-

1. John W. Blassingame, "American Nationalism and Other Loyalties in the Soutern Colonies, 1763–1775," *Journal of Southern History*, XXXIV (February, 1968), 49–75.

ners, both in spirit and economic interest. And, as is well known, at the Constitutional Convention of 1787, several delegates referred to divisions between North and South. James Madison put the matter most pointedly when he said that "the States were divided into different interests not by their difference in size, but by other circumstances; the most material of which resulted partly from climate, but principally from the effects of their having or not having slaves. The two concurred in forming the great division of interests in the United States. It did not lie between the large and small States; it lay between the Northern and Southern." It is worth recalling, however, that at the time Madison was speaking, Pennsylvania, New Jersey, and New York still had slavery. We cannot be sure, therefore, that Madison's "South" was only the South as we would define it today. However, George Mason, Madison's Virginia colleague at the convention, clarified the matter some when he asserted that "the Northern states have an interest different from the five Southern states." [2] It would seem, therefore, that even at that early date slavery was identified with the South alone, despite the legal existence of the institution in almost all of the other newly independent states.

Also in the late 1780s, Thomas Jefferson drew up a list of adjectives to describe the nature of the North and the South to a foreign correspondent. In the North, he wrote, the people "are cool, sober, laborious, persevering, independent, jealous of their own liberties, chicaning, superstitious and hypocritical in their religion." In the South, he went on, "they are fiery, voluptuary, indolent, unsteady, independent, zealous of their own liberties, but trampling on those of others, generous, candid, and without attachment or pretentions of any religion

2. Max Farrand (ed.), *The Records of the Federal Convention of 1787* (4 vols.; New Haven: Yale University Press, 1911), I, 486, II, 362–63.

but that of the heart."[3] What is worth noting about this listing of stereotypes is that it comes close to those assigned to southerners and northerners in 1860 and in 1960. Notice, too, the similarity with the aforementioned list of adjectives enunciated by the southern students to differentiate northerners from southerners.

When the new government was formed in 1789, the beginning of identification of the South with slavery was even more clearly evident than it had been in the Constitutional Convention. During the First Congress, a group of Quakers, despite constitutional prohibition, presented a petition for ending the slave trade. (The Constitution provided that no such provision could be enacted for twenty years.) Those southerners who spoke against receiving the petition at all, emphasized the loss of labor to the South if the trade were terminated. Significant, too, was the fact that southerners were not then united on the matter. Madison, for example, was quite willing, unlike many of his fellow southerners, to receive the petition despite its asking for what he recognized was an unconstitutional act. The representatives from Georgia and South Carolina were conspicuous by their adamant refusal to countenance any petition on the subject. William Loughton Smith of South Carolina even mounted a defense of slavery on the ground that Negroes "were an indolent people, improvident, averse to labor; when emancipated they would either starve or plunder," he warned. He closed his lengthy remarks with a quotation from Jefferson's *Notes on Virginia*, to show, as Smith put it, that Negroes were "by nature an inferior race of beings."[4]

3. Letter to Chastellux, September 2, 1785, Julian P. Boyd (ed.), *The Papers of Thomas Jefferson* (Princeton: Princeton University Press, 1953—), VIII, 468.
4. *Annals of the Congress of the United States* (Washington: Gales and Seaton, 1834), 1st Congress, 2nd Session, 1456.

A similar linkage between slavery and the South emerged in the early years of the nineteenth century, during the debates in Congress over the penalties to be placed upon those who violated the 1807 prohibition against the importation of slaves into the United States. As one congressman from Georgia said in opposing the death penalty for importing blacks after 1807, "A large majority of the people of the Southern States do not consider slavery as a crime. They do not believe it immoral to hold human flesh in bondage. More deprecate slavery as an evil," he admitted; "as a political evil; but not as a crime. . . . It is best to be candid on this subject," he advised. "If they considered the holding of men in slavery as a crime, they would necessarily accuse themselves, a thing which human nature revolts at. I will tell the truth. A large majority of people in the Southern States do not consider it as even an evil. Let the gentlemen go and travel in that quarter of the Union." A congressman from North Carolina made the same point, this time referring to the South, not simply the southern states. "The people of the South do not generally consider slavery as a moral offense," he began. "Gentlemen always appear on this subject to blend the question of immorality with that of political expediency. But it is . . . well known that the Negroes imported are brought from a state of slavery. There is only a transfer from one master to another; and it is admitted that the condition of the slaves in the Southern states is much superior to that of those in Africa. Who, then, will say that the trade is immoral?"[5]

As an idea, then, the South, it would seem, clearly existed in the minds of some southerners, at least; and by the early years of the nineteenth century, it was publicly identified with slavery. Yet, it does not seem to have been more than an

5. *Annals of the Congress of the United States* (Washington: Gales and Seaton, 1852), 9th Congress, 2nd Session, 238–40.

idea, a sense of difference rather than a deeply felt or perceived distinction or identification. Not even all southern politicians believed alike on the issue, as their divergent voting patterns and their statements in the course of the debates make evident. Moreover, the doctrine of the limited power of the federal government, which southern defenders of slavery invoked in the Constitutional Convention and later, was considerably eroded, if not abandoned, during the ascendancy of the party of Jefferson in Washington after 1800. It was New England, not the South, that invoked the doctrine of states' rights in those years and spoke for a narrow and circumscribed vision of the nation's power. As Charles Sydnor has shown, during the first two decades of the nineteenth century the South was clearly a part of the national culture. Its Democratic-Republican party—that is, the party of Jefferson—flourished in the North as well as the South. The region participated along with the North in various reform movements like the abolition of imprisonment for debt, temperance, and the expansion of suffrage. The South, moreover, led the nation in the development of public higher education, with Georgia, North Carolina, and South Carolina anticipating all of the northern states in founding state universities. Even the number of antislavery societies in the South as late as 1820 exceeded that in the northern states. And the Athenses, Spartas, Romes, and Troys that began to appear on the maps of southern and northern states alike during these same years measured the common participation of the two sections in the classical revival.

The lack of a common political identification among the southern states was succinctly measured in the vote over the Bonus Bill in 1817. The bill would have used funds obtained from the newly chartered Second Bank of the United States to build roads and other internal improvements under federal direction. Southern congressmen split down the middle: 23 against and 22 for; the Middle Atlantic states voted heavily for: 47 to 19; while New England assumed the most narrowly sectional position: 34 against and only 8 in favor.

The turning point in the outlook of the southern states came in the 1820s. Beginning with the Panic of 1819 and the debates over the admission of Missouri, southern states began a return to that sense of identity that their years in national power and the absence of threats to southern interests had rendered dormant. I say a return because I think Charles Sydnor's argument that southern identity began to form only with the 1820s ignores the evidence of previous self-consciousness that we have already noticed in the years before the War of 1812. In fact, some of Sydnor's own evidence for southern hostility toward the North or the East seems actually to show that only a bout with economic adversity was necessary to bring out a sense of difference that had been there all along. Sydnor tells us that northern peddlers were accused in newspapers during the Panic of 1819 of selling southerners things they did not need and thus were perceived as draining the South's wealth. Although Sydnor cites such evidence to show how the Panic aroused southern suspicions of the North, thus helping to create a sense of southern identity, it is more likely that the antagonism was there already, for the activities of northern peddlers were hardly to be taken seriously as a significant cause for the South's economic difficulties. Moreover, as Sydnor admits, the social and political conflicts within the southern states over what to do about the Panic were more disruptive than unifying, for in state after state there were hard-fought struggles over stay laws, paper money, and banks. Such internal conflicts were hardly a source of southern unity or of an antagonism between North and South. The Panic, in short, should be seen at best as a precipitating factor, rather than as a causal element in the growth of southern self-consciousness.

A much more powerful manifestation of hostility between the sections, and of southern identification with slavery, is found in the Missouri crisis of 1819–1821. Certainly the effort on the part of some northerners to keep the territory of Missouri from becoming a state until it prohibited slavery united the southern states as nothing before had done. Yet even during those debates earlier arguments about states' rights and slavery were picked up as often as new defenses of slavery and the South were raised. What does stand out is that in the course of the Missouri debates southerners other than South Carolinians and Georgians pressed the identification of the South with slavery. That Thomas Jefferson, for example, who had been for so long publicly doubtful about the merits of slavery, should now talk privately about disunion if Missouri could not enter the Union with slavery is a striking measure of how far otherwise-liberal southerners had come down the road that led to the identification of the South's destiny with slavery.

The familiar question of what motivations or intentions lay behind the northern attempt to prohibit slavery in Missouri is not a prime concern here. Yet seeking an answer to that question does throw some further light on the origins of southern distinctiveness. A number of historians have traced the impetus behind the northern action to resentment over the clause in the Constitution that permitted slaves to be counted in apportioning the House of Representatives. This basis of apportionment gave the South an advantage that the free-labor North lacked. Still other historians have contended that hostility between the sections arose because of the different economic interests of the North and South. Both arguments oversimplify the matter. Despite the South's overrepresentation because of the three-fifths clause for counting slaves in the population, the North's predominance in the House was established at the First Congress and its numerical superiority only increased with each census thereafter. Moreover, at the time of the Missouri controversy, the interests of the North were not clearly industrial—New England, for example, still opposed protective tariffs—and the South, as the vote on the Bonus Bill revealed, was hardly united. Northern hostility toward, or jealousy of, the South was certainly there, but it was not based on such obvious things. Expressions of that hostility even antedate the Missouri debates of 1820. As early as 1801 one New Englander wrote, "There is a spirit of domination engrafted on the character of the Southern people. Of all the inhabitants of this continent," he contended, "they are the most imperious in their manners."[6] If slavery's effect upon southerners seems to be implied in this criticism of the South, some historians have turned the matter around and traced New England's later opposition to slavery to an old hostility toward the South. "That many sons of Federalist fathers assumed leading roles in the abolitionist crusade after 1815 was certainly not coincidental," writes James Banner in his study of New England Federalists. "When they entered the battle with the slave masters, they rehearsed once again the principles of their fathers' politics and fought as much against the South and for New England as against slavery and for the slave."[7] Whatever the origins or roots of that northern hostility, it was certainly there at the time of the Missouri debates. It was evident in the unrestrained rejoicing among northern

6. Quoted in Linda K. Kerber, *Federalists in Dissent: Imagery and Ideology in Jeffersonian America* (Ithaca: Cornell University Press, 1970), 25–26.

7. James M. Banner, Jr., *To the Hartford Convention: The Federalists and the Origins of the Party Politics in Massachusetts, 1789–1815* (New York: Alfred A. Knopf, 1970), 108–109.

congressmen and in the northern states generally when an antislavery northerner was elected Speaker of the House in 1821. It is not without significance in this regard, too, that of the eighteen northern congressmen who voted with the South or failed to vote against the Compromise of 1820, only five were reelected. That would not be the last time that hostility toward southerners—aside from hostility toward slavery—would appear in the politics that was the context of the South's course to distinctiveness. Nor would those defeats of prosouthern northerners be the last occasion in which a sense of southern identity would be fostered by the knowledge that northern friends of the South suffered at home because of that friendship.

The Missouri crisis was at once the identification of slavery as the basis of southern difference and a measure of the depth of southern identity. On the question of whether Missouri ought to be allowed to retain slavery, there was no dissent at all among southern congressmen. Southerners in Congress divided only on whether a line ought to be drawn to prohibit slavery anywhere in the Louisiana Purchase in the future. Some southerners were already prepared to break from the Union if slavery were excluded in Missouri; all southerners in Congress saw slavery as an institution with which they identified their region and one that ought not be limited in the future.[8]

The Missouri crisis was merely the first of a series of instances in which the southern states learned to rely upon a narrow construction of the Constitution to protect themselves against what they considered outside threats. It was during the 1820s, for example, that the southern states began to con-

8. Glover, Moore, *The Missouri Controversy, 1819–1821* (Lexington: University of Kentucky Press, 1953), has been invaluable in arriving at these conclusions.

sider the tariff from a regional standpoint and to find the protective tariff a threat to their burgeoning cotton economy. As recently as 1816 a substantial minority of southern states had supported a mildly protective tariff. But during the early 1820s, as the South became overwhelmingly committed to cotton, some southern politicians began to advance the novel constitutional argument that a protective tariff was contrary to the Constitution and therefore beyond the power of Congress.

If the agricultural exporting economy of the South encouraged the region to oppose a protective tariff, the geography of the South allowed it to extend the strict construction of the Constitution to the question of federal support for internal improvements. Unlike the western interior of the country, the South had no pressing need for the construction of new transportation lines, since it was already well served by nature with a network of rivers and a long coastline. Albert Fishlow has pointed out that even as late as 1908, some five thousand miles of internal waterways in the South were still designated as navigable. The South, Fishlow adds, was an exporter of staples long before there were internal improvements fostered by the federal government.[9] Southerners thus, unlike westerners, could indulge their constitutional principles without seriously jeopardizing their economic future.

In the case of the disputes with the southern Indians, southerners found strict construction of the Constitution or states' rights not only in line with their interests, but a way of positively advancing their interests. By invoking the doctrine of states' rights against the federal government, Georgia, Alabama, and Mississippi during the 1820s and early 1830s gained access to Indian lands within their borders that other-

9. Albert Fishlow, *American Railroads and the Transformation of the Antebellum Economy* (Cambridge, Mass.: Harvard University Press, 1965), 84–85.

wise would have been closed to white settlement for decades to come. Charles Sydnor is quite right when he argues that in the course of the 1820s the leaders of a number of southern states learned the value of strict construction and states' rights as a defense or advancement of southern economic and social interests.

What also needs to be recognized, however, is that even at the close of the decade of the 1820s the South was still not united on the issue of the tariff, internal improvements, or the Indians. When South Carolina made its bid to nullify the Tariff of 1832, for example, not a single southern state supported the move. Indeed, Mississippi and Alabama, despite their commitment to both cotton and slavery, specifically repudiated the doctrine of nullification. The Alabama legislature denounced nullification as "unsound in theory and dangerous in practice" and said that "as a remedy it is unconstitutional and essentially revolutionary, leading in its consequences to anarchy and civil discord and finally to the dissolution of the Union." The Mississippi legislature was no less hostile, concluding that the "doctrine of Nullification is contrary to the letter and spirit of the Constitution, and in direct conflict with the welfare, safety and independence of every State in the Union; and to no one of them would its consequences be more deeply disastrous, more ruinous than to the State of Mississippi." [10] On the same occasion, southerners like James Madison argued that the protective tariff was neither unconstitutional nor oppressive to the South. Still other southerners, like President Andrew Jackson and Joel Poinsett of South Carolina, used their influence and power to

10. The replies of the southern states are gathered in Herman V. Ames (ed.), *State Documents on Federal Relations: The States and the United States* (6 vols.; Philadelphia: University of Pennsylvania Press, 1902), IV, 49–50, 53.

defeat South Carolina's nullification of the tariff at the point of agitation.

Even in later years, when the issue of the tariff came up again, it was clear that the South was not united. Kentucky and Louisiana, for example, always showed an interest in a protective tariff if only because their staples—hemp and sugar, respectively—required protection for foreign competition. Some southern states may have learned that a narrow, literal interpretation of the Constitution, with an emphasis upon states' rights, was a way of defending the South's interests in the national forum, but the invocation of the principle was neither automatic nor general. And the reason it was not is that not all southern states had common interests in this respect. On only one question were southerners united. As the fight over the admission of Missouri showed, southern unity prevailed only in regard to the perpetuation of slavery.

So strong was southern concern over slavery that in its behalf even strict construction of the Constitution could be compromised. William Freehling has shown that behind the tariff controversy of the 1820s, which culminated in South Carolina's nullification in 1832, lay the question of slavery. Freehling's argument is that South Carolinians came to oppose the protective tariff not only because it threatened their exporting economy, but primarily because if they could limit federal power in regard to the tariff they would forestall, reduce, or even eliminate the possibility of such power being used against slavery. Freehling's contention is reinforced when it is recognized that twice during the 1820s many southerners abandoned their growing commitment to a strict construction of the Constitution (but not states' rights) when that seemed necessary in order to defend slavery. This willingness to work both sides of the constitutional street reveals that a concern for the future of slavery was at least as important in southerners' minds as was abstract constitutional principle.

The first occasion was in 1821 when Missouri, as part of the Compromise, was permitted to keep in its new constitution the prohibition against migration of free Negroes into the state, despite the explicit guarantee in the United States Constitution for free movement of citizens from one state to another. (Negroes may not have been recognized as citizens in the slave states, but they were so recognized in several northern states.) The second occasion was in 1822 when South Carolina passed the Negro Seamen's Act, providing for the confinement to their ships or to jail of Negro seamen from any state or nation while their vessels were in South Carolina's ports. The impetus behind the law was the Denmark Vesey slave plot of 1822. Vesey was a free Negro who encouraged and organized a slave uprising in Charleston that was only narrowly nipped in the bud. The new law was intended to make more difficult the kind of contact between free blacks and slaves that had almost made real one of the most terrible nightmares of the slave south. A southern-born United States attorney-general, as well as a southern-born federal judge, declared such interference with the freedom of citizens of other nations—not to mention of other states—a violation of the clause in the Constitution that made treaties a part of the supreme law of the land. Again and again Great Britain protested the law, but South Carolina neither repealed nor amended the act, though its refusal hardly represented a strict construction of the Constitution. In time, Georgia, Alabama, Louisiana, North Carolina, and Florida passed similar laws.

What emerges from these contradictions between constitutional principles and behavior when slavery was threatened or perceived to be threatened was that slavery was recognized by leading southerners as central to their society. And this recognition came long before northern abolitionists began their attacks upon the morals of slaveholders. If ever the Jeffersonian hope that slavery would one day disappear from the new Republic had been a reality, by the late 1820s it was no longer seriously entertained. The unity of the South on the admission of Missouri as a slave state was one sign. More symbolic but no less revealing was the outright repudiation by southern representatives in Congress of the effort by some northerners to bring about the gradual ending of slavery by national action at national expense.

The story can be told briefly, though the full story still awaits its historian. In 1824 the Ohio legislature recommended that Congress and the other states consider a plan for the gradual emancipation of slaves and their colonization abroad as they became free. The costs of the scheme were to be borne by the federal government "upon the principle that the evil of slavery is a national one," as the resolution said. Within a year and a half, eight northern states endorsed that plan, all from the West and the Middle Atlantic regions. In 1825 Rufus King of New York introduced a resolution in the United States Senate proposing the creation of a special fund from the sale of public lands to carry out the idea. The reaction from some of the southern representatives was so harsh, writes Charles Sydnor, as "hardly to be explained." [11] Although anemic versions of the plan were advanced in subseqent years, never again, after that initial southern rebuff, were they taken seriously.

The significance of the rejection is not that the proposal was another of those "might-have-beens" of history. In fact, it is most unlikely that the intractable problem of slavery and race in America could have been solved so rationally and so

11. Charles S. Sydnor, *The Development of Southern Sectionalism 1819–1848* (Baton Rouge: Louisiana State University Press, 1948), 151.

easily. Moreover, since removal of free Negroes and former slaves from the United States was a part of the plan, the idea was unacceptable if carried out by force and quite impractical if left up to the voluntary compliance of blacks. By 1820 the vast majority of slaves had been born in the United States, and very few would willingly have accepted removal to a land that was unknown to them. No, the significance of the southern rejection of compensated emancipation and colonization lies in the recognition that as early as 1825 the South had committed itself so deeply to slavery and that slavery was so imbedded in the South's identity that the region could only view any proposal to end it, however gradually, as an attack upon its being. "The people of this state," resolved the lower house of the South Carolina legislature, "will adhere to a system, descended to them from their ancestors, and now inseparably connected with their social and political existence." [12] Betty Fladeland has recently observed that compensating slaveholders for the emancipation of their slaves was always viewed by defenders of slavery in the South "as a radical rather than as a moderate or reasonable solution to the slavery problem and that they were prepared to resist any plan based on it." [13]

The identification of the South with the institution of slavery is, of course, hardly news. Most historians today accept the centrality of slavery in the evolution of southern sectionalism, the drive to secession, and the War for Southern Independence. The acceptance of slavery in the South, however, had deeper and more enduring consequences than setting the course of the South to secession. It also set the South

12. Quoted *ibid*.
13. Betty Fladeland, "Compensated Emancipation: A Rejected Alternative," *Journal of Southern History*, XLII (May, 1976), 185.

on the course to its modern distinctiveness. It is to that consequence of slavery that we must now turn.

Whether one is interested in the nature of the early antebellum South or of the modern South, the agricultural character of the region is fundamental. Today the South is the most rural region of the nation; in the years before the War for Southern Independence that description was even more appropriate. Although all of the major divisions of the country in 1860 could be spoken of as agricultural, the South easily surpassed all of them in its commitment to farming. About 84 percent of the labor force of the South was engaged in farming 'in 1860, as compared with 40 percent in the remainder of the country. The South constituted slightly less than 40 percent of the population of the United States, but it raised 50 percent of the nation's cattle, 60 percent of the swine, 90 percent of the mules, 50 percent of the corn, 50 percent of the poultry, and 52 percent of the oxen. Only in amounts of wheat, oats, rye, and sheep was the South behind the North in the production of specific major farm products. In the production of the great international staples—tobacco, cotton, sugar, rice, and hemp—the South was not only without peer, but without serious competitors in the North.[14]

The deep and enduring involvement with agriculture and rurality implied by these figures flowed naturally from the South's unique commitment to slavery. Although slave labor was used principally in the production of the great staples, its

14. The standard work on the agricultural economy of the South, from which these and other figures are taken, is Lewis C. Gray, *History of Agriculture in the Southern United States to 1860* (2 vols.; Washington: Carnegie Institution, 1933); see especially pp. 811–12, 831–32. The proportion of the labor force in agriculture is taken from Stanley Lebergott, "Labor Force and Employment, 1800–1960," National Bureau of Economic Research, *Output, Employment, and Productivity in the United States After 1800* (New York: Columbia University Press, 1966), 131.

success in producing those commodities encouraged a general interest in other kinds of agriculture as well. It was slavery, that is labor coerced by law, that made the plantation possible. Given the great demand for the staples, principally cotton, in the international market, it was to be expected that the South would turn to growing cotton and other farm commodities. But neither the strong international demand for cotton nor the readily available land could be taken advantage of fully without slavery. Free men would not work for others at subsistence wages when so much land was available. At the same time, farmers working their individual and necessarily small plots of lands were too few in number to meet the burgeoning demand or to exploit the empty land. It is quite likely that without slavery, the South, because of its hot and humid climate, would have been more slowly populated by Europeans than it was; one thing slavery did was to introduce working people into the region who had no choice about climate or locale. In any event, slavery made the plantation a flourishing form of agricultural organization; slavery in league with the plantation made "mass production" in agriculture possible. In so doing, slavery and the plantation laid the foundation for the South's distinctiveness. No other region of the nation was able to turn slavery to such good use, primarily because no other region was so well suited to the growth of commodities that were in world demand. As David Potter observed, "If cotton fastened slavery on the South . . . slavery fastened cotton upon the South." [15]

As a form of agricultural organization the plantation began in the seventeenth century, with white labor held to the land by law in the form of indentured servitude. But in the colonial era white labor was replaced by black Africans held to the

15. David M. Potter, The Impending Crisis, 1848–1861 (New York: Harper and Row, 1976), 455.

land as slaves. The reason for the replacement does not really concern us here, though it would seem to have been a matter of economics. Slaves, who could be made to work for a lifetime and whose offspring were also slaves were obviously cheaper as laborers than white men and women whose terms as indentured servants were limited and whose children were born free. Whatever the reason for the shift in the racial character of the dependent cultivators, the shift decreed that the South would become the one region of the country in which black people made up a significant part of the population. Other regions of the country had black slaves, but only the South had the plantation and thus the opportunity and incentive to introduce large numbers of slaves into its labor force.

Slavery did much more than determine that the South would be a biracial society. It also shaped the economic and demographic patterns of the South for years to come, chiefly because it was profitable. At one time, historians were not at all sure that slavery as it was practiced in the antebellum South was competitive with free labor. Indeed, the nineteenth-century attack on slavery as a system of labor generally emphasized the allegedly inherent inefficiencies in any labor system that relied upon physical coercion rather than internalized incentives. And even southern historian Ulrich B. Phillips, who was certainly not hostile to the old regime in the South, contended that it was far from a profitable way to make cotton. The argument was not that the slave plantation failed to produce any profit, but rather that the profit it did produce fell far short of that which would have been returned from other kinds of investment. Today, however, there are almost no historians who argue that slavery was unprofitable to the average planter, even though there were certainly individual slaveowners who received only a small or negligible return. Beginning with the seminal article by Alfred Conrad and John Meyer in 1958, economic historians have demonstrated from a variety of sources that on the average the cotton plantations of the South earned on their capital about what would have been received if that same sum had been invested in nonagricultural enterprises outside the South, like northern railroads. Southern planters, in short, were making the best of their economic opportunities when they invested their capital and plowed back their profits into land and slaves to make more cotton.

Certainly there is more than one reason why the South wedded itself to Negro slavery and the plantation. The evidence that on the average slavery produced a good profit for slaveowners suggests that at least one of the reasons for that commitment was that slavery paid. In receiving a handsome return, however, southerners also paid a social price. The slave and the plantation shaped the economy, the society, and the culture in which the white free people lived together with black slaves. And many of the results of that shaping remain today in the persistent distinctiveness of the South, a persistence over the course of a century and a half that is the chief reason for asserting the continuity of southern history.

One of the distinctive aspects of the modern South, as we have seen, is that relatively fewer people from continental Europe and Asia live in the region than in the rest of the United States. That pattern began in the nineteenth century, and it can be related to the success of slavery. Prior to the great immigration of Catholic Irish, Protestant and Catholic Germans, and Protestant Scandinavians in the course of the fourth decade of the nineteenth century, the distribution of peoples in North and South was not conspicuously different. Scots-Irish, Huguenot French, Swiss, and Germans settled among the predominantly English in both regions. And even when large numbers of Germans and Catholic Irish came to the United States in the 1840s and 1850s some did go to the South. Indeed, in cities like Charleston, Memphis, and Louisville immigrants constituted a third or more of the population in 1860. Yet the fact remains that the South became the permanent home of considerably fewer immigrants than the North. In 1860 only 13 percent of the foreign-born in the United States lived in the southern slave states, though the South then embraced almost 40 percent of the population and almost half of the settled area of the country.

How is this antebellum demographic pattern related to slavery and the plantation? At the time and since, some observers have argued that immigrants were antislavery and therefore shunned the slave South. From what we know of the proslavery proclivities of many Irish immigrants in the North, that argument is hardly convincing. It is true that some Germans were vocally antislavery, but, ironically enough, that attitude did not keep them from settling in the South. For it was the antislavery Germans who settled towns like Fredricksburg and New Braunfels in central Texas in order to avoid the slave areas of the state. Attitudes toward slavery cannot explain the immigrants' shunning of the South. A more plausible explanation is the lack of economic opportunities in the region. To European immigrants who expected to farm in the United States the opportunities in the South must have been perceived as limited. The plantation would have been seen as a highly competitive rival to free labor, a rival that was absent from the Northwest. Moreover, a slave society must have appeared aristocratic and therefore undemocratic to people fleeing the class distinctions and aristocratic pretensions of old Europe.

One reason for believing that the plantation was perceived as, and was in fact, disadvantageous to potential yeoman farmers is that the South was a net exporter of people. In 1860 some 800,000 more white southerners lived outside the southern states than northerners lived in the South. This difference suggests that slavery, by legally holding Negroes in labor, was actually overpopulating the region. Since the Negro slaves could not leave, the whites did. Moreover, the recent work of Sam Hilliard and Robert Gallman, arguing for self-sufficiency in food on the large plantations, suggests another way in which small farmers suffered from the existence of slavery and the plantation in the South. In the South small farmers would not have had as wide a local market for their foodstuffs as they would have had in a small-farmer, small-town economy such as was developing simultaneously in the Old Northwest. For that reason immigrants who intended to be farmers would more likely have been attracted to the Northwest than to the South.

Immigrants also chose not to settle in the antebellum South because opportunities in cities and factories were considerably fewer there than in the North. It is true, as Leonard Curry has recently shown, that the proportion of the nation's large cities in the South in 1850 was about the same as the region's proportion of the national population. Yet the fact remains that of the fifteen slave states only Maryland, Delaware, and Louisiana—because of New Orleans—contained a proportion of their populations living in cities equal to that of the nation at large.[16] The South lagged behind the nation then, as it does today, in proportion of urbanized population. Everyone recognized that New York, Pennsylvania, and New England were more highly urbanized than the South in the antebellum years. It is less well recognized, however, that

16. Leonard Curry, "Urbanization and Urbanism in the Old South: A Comparative View," *Journal of Southern History*, XL (February, 1974), 43–60.

those states of the South—Kentucky, Tennessee, Alabama, and Mississippi—which were settled at roughly the same time as Ohio, Indiana, and Illinois were less than half as urbanized. In 1860 Illinois and Indiana counted forty cities over 2,500 population; at that same date seven states of the Deep South counted only thirty-three such cities altogether. Immigrants who were without funds for buying or starting a farm and who looked, therefore, to the cities of America for a chance to begin life anew, or to accumulate savings for buying a farm later on, were not likely to look to the South. (Why the South had fewer cities is a question I will return to when we consider why the South lacked a significant degree of manufacturing.)

Another explanation sometimes given for the shunning of the South by immigrants is that migrants from one continent to another typically tend to follow established lines of transportation. Since the canal and railroad lines from New York City generally led west, not south, it followed that immigrants would tend to go west on the Hudson River–Erie Canal–Great Lakes waterway or by railroad after 1850. To go south required special knowledge and complicated travel arrangements, not to mention a willingness to accept a climate quite different from that of northern Europe.

Persuasive as the trade-routes argument might be for New York, Boston, or Philadelphia, it does not explain why most immigrants landed at northern ports. After all, Norfolk, Charleston, Savannah, Mobile, and New Orleans were quite accessible to Europe by ocean ships. The explanation, of course, is that the southern ports were usually not in direct and regular shipping communication with Europe. The reason that there was little direct shipping between southern ports and Europe can also be attributed to the economy that was based upon the slave plantation. Certainly southern leaders desired direct trade with Europe, if only to save the cost of insurance, transshipment, and storage in New York City on their trade with Europe. Again and again southern leaders called for the establishment of direct shipping lines to Europe. Why weren't these efforts successful? Southern markets did not justify such lines. American law prohibited foreign ships from engaging in the coastal trade; for a southern port to maintain a direct shipping line it had to generate sufficient business to justify a line's going only to and from a single American port. Inasmuch as cotton was the principal American export commodity there was never any doubt that outward shipments could easily support a direct line to Europe. It was the relatively small value and volume of the incoming goods that prevented a steady direct trade between Europe and southern ports. Foreign ships did call at southern ports with immigrants, some manufactures, and a good deal of ballast in order to pick up cotton for the return trip. But the connection was irregular or episodic because the few lines that did get established could not survive for long on the limited market provided by the hinterland of the southern ports. Not only was the population less densely settled because of the agricultural economy, but a sizable portion of that population was made up of slaves whose consumption of goods was meager. As a result, the South's importations from Europe generally came through the North, either by inland routes or via the American coastal trade operated by Yankees.

The failure of the South to establish a direct trade with Europe is closely related to its relatively weak development of manufactures as compared with the contemporary North. There was, of course, some manufacturing in the Old South. Clement Eaton has pointed out, for example, that the South's share of total national production of manufactured goods was actually higher in 1860 than in 1900. And during the 1850s the amount of manufacturing in the South rose 43 percent, though the population increased only 20 percent. The work of Richard Griffin has also demonstrated that textile manufacturing in the Old South was considerably more widespread and productive than many historians have maintained. And certainly tobacco and iron manufacturing in Virginia were among the major industrial activities of the country, not only of the region. In the end, however, we cannot escape the fact that in 1860 the South produced less than 15 percent of the nation's manufactures. The amount of capital invested in manufacturing in Indiana and Illinois—two states admitted to the Union at roughly the same time as Alabama and Mississippi and therefore with no temporal advantages—was greater than that of all the seven states of the Deep South extending from South Carolina to Texas.

The relative weakness of manufacturing in the antebellum South, like the failure to develop a direct trade connection with Europe, is related to the peculiarities of an economy shaped by slavery and the plantation. A few years ago economic historian William Parker showed statistically that the southern antebellum economy, because it was based upon slave labor, lacked a middle sector—that is, a portion of the economy in which consumer wants were high, thereby providing a basis for direct trade and for the development of local manufacturing. Parker first calculated the per-capita annual income for free nonslaveholders per square mile for the southern states east of the Mississippi; he then made the same calculations for the nonslaveholding population of the comparably agricultural Northwest. The difference in per-capita income was dramatic: $985 per square mile for the southern states and $2,000 for the middle western states. Since in those years the Old Northwest was primarily agricultural, it is evident from these figures that the demand for manufactures in the South would be less than in the Northwest when related to density as well as population. Fewer towns in the South than in the Northwest meant, Parker added, that the South lacked the small-town industry that would have provided the foundation of skills and technology essential for the development of manufactures for the mass market.[17]

Eugene Genovese has argued that an important reason for the relative lack of manufacturing in the Old South was that the planter class was hostile to manufacturing. Certainly some planters did object to what they considered the wrong kind of development for an agrarian South. But such objections have to incorporate the views of the many spokesmen for the South who advocated more, not less, industrial development. Certainly no one can fault the southern boosterism of J. D. B. DeBow, yet *DeBow's Review*, which he edited from New Orleans, was in the forefront of the movement for economic diversification of the region. The so-called commercial conventions of the 1840s and 1850s organized by southern political and business leaders also pushed vigorously for industry in the South. Leading advocates of a slave South, like Robert Hayne of South Carolina and George Fitzhugh of Virginia, also spoke out in support of the industrial growth of their region.

Moreover, as historians document the versatility of slave labor it becomes increasingly evident that there was little or no intrinsic hostility between slavery and the development of industry. Robert Starobin has shown that slaves worked effectively in all kinds of industrial tasks, sometimes side by side with white workers. The tobacco manufacturing establish-

17. William N. Parker, "Slavery and Southern Economic Development: An Hypothesis and Some Evidence," in W. N. Parker (ed.), *The Structure of the Cotton Economy of the Antebellum South* (Washington: Agricultural History Society, 1970).

ments in Richmond were largely manned by slaves and the very successful Tredegar Iron Works was run with slave labor. Ernest Lander concluded that South Carolina cotton textile mills using slave labor competed quite successfully with those using free white labor until the price of slaves got too high because of the demand from plantation agriculture. In a recent article John E. Stealey has pointed out that in certain industries, notably salt manufacturing in western Virginia, slave labor, precisely because it was coerced labor, could develop southern natural resources that would otherwise have lain dormant for lack of free labor willing or able to work as steadily and as efficiently.[18] One need not go as far as Robert Fogel and Stanley Engerman do in their controversial book *Time on the Cross*, seeing slave labor as more efficient than northern free agricultural labor; but there is no reason to believe that slaves were so inefficient that they could not be profitably employed in manufacturing. The capability of the slave labor force was not a primary reason for the South's failure to develop manufacturing.

On a somewhat different level of analysis, George Green in his thorough study of banking in antebellum Louisiana denies that there was a contradiction between slave society and economic development, as some historians have argued. Income per worker in Louisiana, he points out, was the third highest in the country, and the state's nonagricultural percapita income was the highest in the nation. Green sees Louisiana as making good use of the latest technology, thus challenging the view that innovations were resisted or unappreciated by an allegedly anticapitalist planter-dominated South. In 1838, for example—the only year for which figures are available—Louisiana led the nation in the use of steam

18. John Edmund Stealey III, "Slavery and the Western Virginia Salt Industry," *Journal of Negro History*, LIX (April, 1974), 105–131.

power. Railroad construction in that state also reached a high level in the late antebellum years and was not opposed by planters, as sometimes is argued.

The conclusion that seems to emerge, then, is that slave labor did not move into manufacturing and manufacturing did not develop as rapidly in the South as in the rest of the nation because both capital and labor earned competitive returns from agriculture. Clement Eaton and others have pointed out that during the mild depression in cotton prices during the 1840s manufacturing jumped forward in the South as disenchanted planters shifted capital and labor in search of a better return. Then when cotton prices turned upward in the 1850s, the growth in manufacturing slackened. It was, one may conclude, the comparative advantage of the South in growing certain crops, particularly cotton, that kept its capital and labor concentrated in agriculture.

Some commentators have talked loosely about capital being tied up in slaves in the antebellum South, thus preventing the development of manufacturing. This argument, however, was effectively answered a number of years ago by Kenneth Stampp when he pointed out that slaveholders could easily have shifted their holdings into cash and manufacturing, for there was always a steady market for slaves. Moreover, once the foreign slave trade was closed, the purchase of slaves by a planter did not cause the South to lose his expenditure, for the money remained within the region though now it was in the hands of the trader or the seller of the slave. Either could have invested in manufacturing if that had seemed competitive with slaves or land. Other commentators on the slave South have emphasized the tendency of slaveholders to "waste" their resources on conspicuous consumption, thus limiting capital accumulations for investment in manufacturing. But the careful survey of the sources by Jane Pease makes it difficult to believe that southerners were any more profligate with their incomes than upper class northerners.[19]

The fact seems to be, as Morton Rothstein has pointed out, that many planters were not only interested, but actively engaged in railroading, banking, ginning, and manufacturing of all kinds.[20] Given this diversity of economic interests among the planters, particularly those of the Deep South where the so-called "essence" of the slave economy was located, it is hard to see them as anticapitalist either in outlooks or actions. Indeed, that seems to be the more reasonable conclusion to draw from Eugene Genovese's enumeration of planters who were active in nonagricultural enterprises, which he set forth in his book *The Political Economy of Slavery.* These men were not planters dominating industrialists, as he argues, but capitalist-planters seeking a good return on their surplus earnings gained from agriculture.

Although the planters were not anticapitalist or pre-bourgeois in their outlook, as Genovese contends (I will say more about this question later), it would be a mistake to assume that men and women who lived on great agricultural estates in intimate relationship with workers and servants would not develop a different relationship with their workers than men and women whose daily lives were spent in cities and in much more impersonal relationship with their employees. Masters and slaves lived and worked on the same plantation, for the absentee planter was a rarity in the Old

19. Jane H. Pease, "A Note on Patterns of Conspicuous Consumption among Seaboard Planters, 1820–1860," *Journal of Southern History,* XXXV (August, 1969), 381–93.

20. Morton Rothstein, "The Cotton Frontier of the Antebellum United States: A Methodological Battleground," in Parker (ed.), *The Structure of the Cotton Economy,* 161. See Also Stanley L. Engerman, "A Reconsideration of Southern Economic Growth, 1770–1860," *Agricultural History,* XLIX (April, 1975), 343–61, for more recent references and arguments in the same direction.

South. Under such circumstances there were certainly opportunities for greater cruelty and oppression, but there were also
greater opportunities for paternalism, personal contact, and
sometimes affection between master and slave than in northern cities where work and residence were usually separated
and workers and employers met mainly at the job.

Southern society also differed from northern in that the
social hierarchy culminated in the planter, not the industrialist. The planter-status was more than the top of the social
pyramid; it was the ideal to which other white southerners
aspired. Maunsel White, for example, who was a very successful merchant in New Orleans in the 1850s crowned his
life in his own eyes as well as his neighbors' by becoming a
sugar planter in his declining years. Mere wealth, if accumu-
lated from trade, was not sufficient to bestow the final ac-
colade of success. Nor was it enough to be simply a planter.
For as Daniel Hundley, the antebellum South's prime contemporary commentator on social mobility, pointed out in
1860, those southern planters who seemed to cherish money
more than other social values were quickly stigmatized as
"Southern Yankees." This was all a part of the Old South's
myth of gentility, which northerners as well as southerners
voiced, elaborated upon, and seemed to believe. But for a society that was still largely frontier even in 1860 and hardly
more than a single generation removed from personal and
immediate contact with hoe and plow, the myth was more as-
piration than a reflection of social reality. The rough and tum-
ble frontier life that leaps off the pages of Longstreet's *Georgia
Scenes* and Baldwin's *Flush Times in Alabama and Mississippi* or that is reflected in the antics of George W. Harris' Sut
Lovingood and Johnson Hooper's Simon Suggs is hard to reconcile with the life in the Big House in Margaret Mitchell's
Gone With the Wind. Both levels of social life occurred in the

Old South, to be sure. But even in *Gone With the Wind* it is clear that the planters' gentility and cultivation of aristocratic ways were very new and only lightly rooted in a South still largely in the process of becoming. Moreover, Daniel Hundley's picture of the "Southern gentleman" as one who scorned money-making and business is quite at variance with the respectable record of production and earnings that we have seen was characteristic of antebellum southern agriculture. Such successes are not achieved by left-handed attention to business. The planters may have lived on rural estates and surrounded themselves with the marks of leisured existence, but their economic achievements assure us that they were, as a class, not wanting in entrepreneurial and managerial skills. The agricultural nature of the plantation may have bestowed an antiurban bias upon southern culture, but that bias was no more a different world view from that of the North than William Jennings Bryan's later distrust of the city constituted a different world view from Mark Hanna's.

One of the most profound, if obvious, consequences of slavery was that it locked the South into an agricultural economy in which the city was minor and the immigrant a relative rarity. The pattern of life begun under slavery persisted beyond emancipation. It persisted for a variety of reasons, but not least among them was the success of agriculture in the antebellum years.

The slave plantation society had additional consequences for southern distinctiveness. It helped to shape a myth of the Old South, which persisted long after slavery was gone and forgotten. As already noted, among southerners there was a myth of the southern gentleman, graciously and hospitably presiding over his broad fields and contented slaves, bringing culture and political leadership to a loyal electorate. This myth of the Old South extended to the North as well, as William Taylor demonstrated in his book *Cavalier and Yankee*. To some northerners, Taylor pointed out, the South represented that which their own region lacked; it was a land of gentility, of concern for personal relations and obligations, the very opposite of the money-grubbing commercialism that seemed to be increasingly the emblem of the contemporary North. Lacking the North's burgeoning cities, multiplying factories, and rising tide of immigrants, the South was easily perceived as an alternative to all that was considered unattractive in the North. In fact, it was easy for northerners to see almost anything they wanted in the South, since few bothered to visit the South to check on the reality.

John Hope Franklin's recent study of southern travelers in the North notes that the heavy movement of southerners to the North for business, travel, pleasure, and just plain curiosity was largely a one-way operation. Northerners, he writes, "seemed to have no interest in looking at the South firsthand. . . . Some businessmen visited southern centers of commerce, and some of them remained for extended periods. But there was no general interest in observing the southern scene *even on the part of northerners who wrote about the South*; and there was no travel in the South comparable to the northern trek made annually by throngs of southerners."[21] Nevertheless, no matter how weakly rooted in reality the northern image of the South may have been, its very existence helped to set the South apart and to enhance its distinctiveness.

There was a second version of the northern view of the South that was even more important in fostering a sense of

21. John Hope Franklin, *A Southern Odyssey: Travelers in the Antebellum North* (Baton Rouge: Louisiana State University Press, 1976), 259. Emphasis added.

difference between the regions. Like the first, it derived from slavery and the plantation. This conception of the South was less idyllic; it was one that emphasized the aristocratic elements in southern life, highlighting the violence, the social pretensions, and the economic backwardness of a slave society. As noted earlier, this northern myth of the slave South began early in the nineteenth century. By the 1850s it was highly developed and widely dispersed in northern society. It was central to the growth of the Republican party, as Eric Foner and other historians have pointed out. The content of the myth was summed up by a Michigan newspaper in 1854, which described southerners as "intolerant, not occasionally, nor by accident,—but habitually and on principle. . . . It is the slave driver's lash, differing little in shape, and applied to Northern white men, instead of Southern slaves, but wielded for the same end, the enforcement of their will, and by essentially the same means—brute force instead of reason and justice." [22] Increasingly, political historians are reminding us that a good bit of the political behavior in the North in the antebellum years is explicable only by reference to the hostility felt toward the South because that region had dominated national politics for so long, and usually in behalf of slavery.

The North's rising hostility toward the South, because it was a slave society, goes a long way to explaining the conservative southern outlook in the antebellum years. Indeed, it can be said that one of the consequences, as well as one of the reinforcements over the years, of the South's distinctiveness is that it has persisted as the most conservative region in the nation. Beginning with the opposition of slavery, the South has continued to be under one kind of attack or another for its

22. Quoted in Ronald P. Formisano, *The Birth of Mass Political Parties: Michigan, 1827–1861* (Princeton: Princeton University Press, 1971), 244.

differences from the rest of the nation. Defensiveness and conservatism have become habits of mind, almost reflexes, so often has the South been flayed for real or imagined deficiencies. The fact of distinctiveness has fed upon itself to the point that it has not been necessary always to specify the bases of that distinctiveness. One has merely to note the tradition of difference in the minds of northerners and southerners. As early as the antebellum years North and South had created a *myth* of difference that went beyond the *facts* of difference. On the eve of secession many southerners had come to use that sense of difference as justification for breaking out of what they considered the procrustean bed of the Union. One writer in the *Southern Literary Messenger* in 1860 traced the roots of the difference to the alleged cavalier origins of Virginia and the assumed roundhead origins of New England. Charles Jones, Jr., wrote his father in January, 1861, from Georgia that he believed "that in this country have arisen two races, which, although claiming a common parentage, have been so entirely separated by climate, by morals, by religion, and by estimates so totally opposite to all that constitutes honor, truth, and manliness, that they cannot longer exist under the same government."[23]

The conservative consequences that stemmed from the need to defend slavery can also be observed in the religious life of southerners. At one time in the early nineteenth century the South contained the beginnings of religious radicalism in the form of Unitarianism. Toward the end of his life Thomas Jefferson said he thought that within a generation

23. See "The Differences of Race between the Northern and Southern People," *Southern Literary Messenger*, XXX (June, 1860), 401–409; Robert Manson Myers (ed.), *Children of Pride: A True Story of Georgia and the Civil War* (New Haven: Yale University Press, 1972), 648.

most young men would be Unitarians. Yet on the eve of the War for Southern Independence, Unitarianism was an overwhelmingly New England sect with no churches in the whole South. What had happened?

The reversal seems to be tied up with the South's need to defend slavery. One of the principal defenses of slavery was to argue that is was in conformity with Scripture, that the ancient Hebrews had held bondsmen without religious objection, and that St. Paul had made quite clear that Christianity similarly had no objection to chattel slavery. Since a literal interpretation of the Bible gave little or no support to an abolitionist position, it is not surprising that antislavery people in order to use Christianity *against* slavery resorted to an interpretative or metaphorical exegesis of the Bible. It is not accidental, therefore, that southerners should become increasingly fond of a literal interpretation of the Bible, just as they found a narrow construction of the Constitution useful in defending slavery. Under such constraints a highly interpretative form of Christianity like Unitarianism could hardly have flourished in the late antebellum South.

A southern conservatism born of the need to defend slavery was manifest, too, in attitudes toward reform in general. The antebellum years constituted a veritable ferment of reform in the United States, in which, during the first two decades of the nineteenth century, the South participated. But under the impact of the need to defend slavery against an increasingly hostile northern and world opinion, southerners found advocacy of reform potentially threatening. To open up to challenge any facet of the social order might well cause slavery itself to be brought into question or placed under attack. Nor was the reasoning wholly paranoid. If a southern eye were cast northward it was plain that many reformers who were active in behalf of women's rights, the peace movement, or new community organizations, were generally also antislavery in their outlook.

The roots of modern southern social conservatism, then, must be traced to the antebellum defense of slavery. Even if the defenders of the institution did not always accept the positive view of slavery, they could not ignore slavery's central place in the society and economy. Hence they were driven to defend it against any criticism that might threaten its survival in a world that was fast moving toward outright hostility to it. What slavery began, other elements of the South's minority status in the nation perpetuated when the peculiar institution had passed into oblivion. That the beginnings were then, however, seems clear.

Similarly, the reputation of the South as a land of violence can be traced to antebellum slavery. John Hope Franklin in his *The Militant South* has pointed out that until the 1820s the South had a reputation that was decidedly not militaristic, principally because the region's Revolutionary War record was considered undistinguished. But the War of 1812, the wars against the southern Indians, and especially the South's prominent role in the Mexican War changed all that. In the heyday of the antebellum years, the South was perceived as the most militaristic section of the country. The charge that the South sent proportionately more sons to West Point than any other section cannot withstand scrutiny. Yet at the time many northerners and southerners believed that assertion, and certainly the impression was reinforced by the South's disproportionately large number of private military academies. Southerners themselves, at the outbreak of hostilities in 1861, boasted that their training as hunters and horsemen in a rural, plantation society insured their superiority to urban northerners on the field of battle.

Other forms of violence were also associated with the South in the antebellum years. At one time the duel had been no more a southern than a northern activity, as the most famous duel in American history on the cliffs along the Hudson River reminds us. But by the last years of the antebellum period, the duel was as closely identified with the South as slavery was. And this was true despite the fact that most southern states, like the northern states, had outlawed the practice. A part of the South's recourse to individual retaliation for injuries, especially those of "honor," can be traced to its rural character; but as we have already noted, that rural character was closely related to slavery. A rural, frontier society is less easy to control socially than a more densely settled one, and that is especially true when the tradition of that frontier has been violent as it has been in the United States.

Slavery itself contributed quite directly to making the South violent, as Charles Sydnor showed years ago. On several counts, Sydnor remarked, slavery weakened the rule of law in the antebellum South. Since slaves could not testify against white men even when they were witnesses to crimes, injustice sometimes went unpunished by the normal processes of the law, thus encouraging men to take into their own hands the punishment of wrongdoers. The normal process of the law might be ignored or pushed aside, too, because slaves were personal property as well as human beings. Masters generally preferred—and the law generally encouraged them—to handle the disciplining of their own slaves, a practice that fostered a general willingness to settle other matters without recourse to law.

The ending of slavery did not end this tendency toward extra-legal action. In fact, it can be said that emancipation reinforced and extended it. From the beginning, after all, slavery had been much more than a form of labor; it was always a way of subordinating black people in a society that feared and hated them. When slavery was abolished the problem of controlling blacks became more, rather than less insistent. Once they were citizens, blacks could no longer be legally coerced or punished differently from other citizens. Yet the whites' desire to keep them "in their place" remained as strong as ever. Throughout the post-Reconstruction years, the high incidence of lynching in the South—reaching a figure of two hundred a year in the 1890s—not to mention other kinds of violence against blacks, testify to the extra-legal ways used by whites to control Negroes who had once been controlled by slavery. Violence against blacks was hardly unknown in the North during these years, as the running down and killing of free Negroes during the Civil War draft riots forcefully remind us. But the simple fact of numbers made a difference. Almost 95 percent of all blacks in the United States lived in the South, thus presenting a considerably larger problem of control than whites in the North ever faced. It was slavery and the agricultural society slavery fostered, it will be remembered, that insured that blacks would remain a substantial part of the population of the South.

Some historians have been so impressed by the way in which slavery shaped the lives of southerners, both white and black, that they have talked not only about southern distinctiveness, but about a uniquely southern world view spawned by slavery. What these commentators mean by a different world view is that southerners, because of their involvement with slavery, exhibited and acted upon a system of values that were quite different from those which other Americans lived by. Eugene Genovese has been the leading proponent of this view. Others, like C. Vann Woodward, as we have already noted, consider antebellum southern culture so intertwined with slavery that the ending of the institution is perceived as a major break in the continuity of southern history. Already, in looking at the economy of the Old South, I have argued in effect that the economic rationality and high rate of return of the slave economy belies any fundamental difference between North and South in economic values. The question of different world views, nonetheless, bears further examination, because it is central to the issue of the continuity of southern history. For if the Old South did develop a different world view from that of the North because of slavery, then it would follow that the overthrow of the slave system during the Civil War would mark a significant break in the flow of southern history. Since my thesis is that continuity is more characteristic than discontinuity, we must now examine critically the argument that the antebellum South developed a different world view from that of the rest of the United States.

III The Limited Distinctiveness of the Old South

AMONG THOSE who have examined the culture and society of the Old South, no one has been more conspicuous in asserting the sharp divergence between the South and the North before the Civil War than Eugene Genovese. It is he who has dramatized the difference by introducing the concept of world view in referring to the culture of the antebellum South. In his book *The World the Slaveholders Made* (1969) he succinctly set forth his conception. "Slavery grew in the South to meet the needs of the world market, but it simultaneously extruded a ruling class with economic interests, political ideals, and moral sentiments, antagonistic to the bourgeoisie dominating that market." Or, as he put it in another place in the same book, the Old South "nurtured a ruling class with a world view setting it apart from the mainstream of capitalist development."[1] The antebellum South, thanks to slavery, developed a culture significantly divergent from the rest of the United States.

Superficially, Genovese's view may not appear very different from that which has been advanced herein. Slavery is seen as compelling social and economic relations to conform to its needs as a functioning and living social institution. Actually, Genovese's and my interpretation of the Old South dif-

1. Eugene D. Genovese, *The World the Slaveholders Made* (New York: Pantheon Books, 1969), 169, 33.

fer in two important respects. Genovese sees the culture of the South as reflecting a system of values fundamentally different from that of the rest of the United States. I do not. I certainly believe that the South was and is a distinctive region, but at the same time I think its system of values—then, as now— was quite congruent with that of the rest of the country. What set the South apart in the antebellum years was its commitment to slavery, but that commitment did not produce a world view significantly different from that of the contemporary North. In short, there were rather narrow limits to the distinctiveness of the Old South. Genovese, on the other hand, sees the differences between the two regions as fundamental, being nothing less than the differences between a bourgeois and a prebourgeois social and intellectual order. The second point on which I dissent from Genovese's conception of the antebellum South is in regard to his class interpretation. He contends that the social engine or force shaping southern society and culture in the years before the Civil War was the pursuit by the planter class of its particular needs and interests. I do not think that a class analysis, as Genovese defines it, fits the evidence we now have on the antebellum South.

Because Genovese's interpretation of the slave South has been highly influential among historians of the South, my reasons for rejecting it will be set forth at some length. I hope simultaneously to make clear the limits as well as the extent of southern distinctiveness in the antebellum years.

As a professed Marxist, Genovese places class interest and class conflict at the root of social development and change. "[T]he decisive element in historical development from a Marxian point of view," he has written, "is class struggle." [2]

2. Eugene D. Genovese, *In Red and Black: Marxian Explorations in Southern and Afro-American History* (New York: Pantheon Books, 1971), 324.

The antebellum South, however, is not an apt example on which to apply concepts of class rule or class struggle. That classes existed in the Old South there can be no doubt, as there can be no doubt that classes existed in the North, or that they exist in the United States today. We know, for instance, that slaveholding families made up only a quarter of all white families in the South and that among slaveholders only a small minority held a preponderance of the slaves. In 1850, for example, 27 percent of the slaveholders owned 75 percent of the slaves. We also know, from the work of Gavin Wright, that the slaveholders as a group held a disproportionate share of the arable land in the South, strongly suggesting that there was not only a concentration of chattel wealth, but also a higher concentration of land ownership than obtained in the agricultural Old Northwest, where there was no slavery. Given the ability of slavery to hold labor to the land, it is not surprising that land should be more highly concentrated in the South than in the North, where hired labor was considerably harder to come by. Without labor there was little advantage to holding large amounts of land. Even so, a comparison between an agricultural state in the North and one in the South shows a very similar degree of concentration of wealth. Richard Lowe and Randolph Campbell have recently reported on their study of wealth holding in Wisconsin and Texas, two states quite comparable in age and economic character. They found that the richest 2.2 percent of Texas families owned 32.2 percent of the wealth of the state, which included slaves, and the richest 2 percent of Wisconsin's adult males owned 31 percent. Gavin Wright has pointed out that the concentration of wealth in the South was probably less than in the cities of the North.[3] Actually, an urban and industrial civilization,

3. Richard Lowe and Randolph Campbell, "Slave Property and the Distribution of Wealth in Texas, 1860," *Journal of American History*, LXIII

as the Northeast was becoming during the 1850s, has always shown higher concentrations of wealth than rural ones, including those resting on slavery and the plantation. It can be further demonstrated, from an analysis of the figures provided by Ralph Wooster, that slaveholders in the states of the Deep South were highly overrepresented in officeholding. In 1850, for example, 48 percent of the members of the Alabama legislature were slaveholders with ten or more slaves each, though only 10 percent of white males twenty years of age and over held that many slaves. For Georgia the figures were roughly the same; and for South Carolina 66 percent of the members of the legislature held that many slaves, though that class in society made up about 15 percent of the white males twenty years and over.[4]

These observations and figures make plain that slaveholders held more power than their numbers warranted. In that sense the Old South was a class society, just as the contemporary North was, though there slaveholding would not have been an appropriate measure of wealth. Real estate and industrial and mercantile capital assets would be the northern measures. That the South was a stratified society or that

_____

(September, 1976). See also Gavin Wright, "'Economic Democracy' and the Concentration of Agricultural Wealth in the Cotton South, 1850–1860," in William N. Parker (ed.)., The Structure of the Cotton Economy of the Antebellum South (Washington: Agricultural History Society, 1970), 63–94.

4. I have calculated these percentages from the figures provided in Ralph Wooster, The People in Power: Courthouse and Statehouse in the Lower South, 1850–1860 (Knoxville: University of Tennessee Press, 1969), and from the population statistics in the census of 1850. Karl Marx himself recognized that the existence of classes was nothing new. "And now as to myself, no credit is due to me for discovering the existence of classes in modern society or the struggle between them. Long before me bourgeois historians had described the historical development of this class struggle and bourgeois economists the economic anatomy of the classes," he wrote to Joseph Wedemeyer in 1852. Karl Marx and Friedrich Engels, Basic Writings on Politics and Philosophy, edited by Lewis S. Feuer (Garden City, N.Y.: Anchor Books, 1959), 457.

wealth and income were unequally distributed is, of course, not the point that Genovese seeks to make. His contention is that the South was dominated by a slaveholding class whose values and goals became those of the other classes, even though those other classes had different interests. In writing about the law in the Old South in his book *Roll, Jordan, Roll* (1974), Genovese speaks of the ruling class "disciplining" itself and "the other classes of society" through the use of public power. "The juridical system may become, then, not merely an expression of class interest . . . it may become an instrument by which the advanced section of the ruling class imposes its viewpoint upon the class as a whole and the wider society." [5] Since this is an assumption implicit in his class interpretation of history, Genovese does not find it necessary to prove through the marshaling of historical evidence that the world view of the planter class was in fact imposed on other classes. The operative word here is *imposed*, for there can be no question that a proslavery view prevailed in the antebellum South. The question is how the society acquired that particular outlook. In Genovese's scheme it was worked out by the planter class, which then induced or coerced the remainder of the society to accept it.

The failure to show this through the marshaling of evidence cannot be overlooked since there is actually a good deal of evidence that argues, on the contrary, that the slaveholding elite was *not* a self-conscious ruling class as Genovese uses that term. Now it is true that in criticizing Ulrich B. Phillips some years ago, Genovese denied that class-consciousness is necessary to his argument. "Phillips," he writes, "made the careless error of assuming that lack of class consciousness proved lack of class antagonism, but the advocates of a class

5. Eugene D. Genovese, *Roll, Jordan, Roll: The World the Slaves Made* (New York: Pantheon Books, 1974), 27.

view of history and of the doctrine of class struggle are not so naive as to equate consciousness with interest."[6] If that is true, then one wonders why we need to look at documents from the past to find out what people believed, or to ascertain their motives for action. With such an approach, if I understand the point, we know already what class interests must exist, even though members of the class fail to explicate them and their actions do not reveal them. I am reluctant to believe that Genovese subscribes to that position since it would render superfluous any examination of the historical documents, and he has certainly immersed himself in the records of the Old South. Indeed, in more recent writings, Genovese seems to make quite clear his belief that self-consciousness is essential to a class analysis. In an essay on the thought of the Italian Marxist Antonio Gramsci, Genovese quotes approvingly from John Cammett's study of Gramsci: "A social class scarcely deserves the name until it becomes *conscious* of its existence as a class; it cannot play a role in history until it develops a comprehensive world view and a political program."[7] And more recently still, in *Roll, Jordan, Roll*, Genovese makes the same point. Here he is discussing the advanced fraction of the slaveholding class in the Old South as seeking to dominate its class and world by creating "a world view appropriate to a slaveholders' regime." To achieve its goal, "the class as a whole must be brought to a higher understanding of itself— transformed from a class-in-itself, reacting to pressures on its objective position, into a class-for-itself, consciously striving to shape the world in its own image."[8]

6. Eugene D. Genovese, "Race and Class in Southern History: An Appraisal of the Work of Ulrich Bonnell Phillips," *Agricultural History*, XLI (October, 1967), 348.

7. Genovese, *In Red and Black*, 409. Italics in original.

8. Genovese, *Roll, Jordan, Roll*, 27.

All of this, it seems to me, implies a process whereby a self-conscious ruling class compelled, or at least convinced, other classes of society to believe that their system of values or world view was the same as its own. If this concept of the way the Old South society functioned is to be credible then it ought to be capable of being shown from the historical evidence—that is, that there was class antagonism, which the ruling planter class overcame. One of the problems facing those who advance a class-struggle interpretation of southern antebellum history, however, is the dearth of evidence of widespread and fundamental hostility on the part of the nonslaveholding majority toward the slave regime. In an effort to meet this evidential problem Genovese has introduced the concept of hegemony.

By *hegemony* he means that the ruling planter class was able to bring the mass of white southerners to accept the planters' class outlook. In that way, the lack of evidence for fundamental class antagonism in the Old South is accounted for. This approach, however, only pushes the analysis farther back; for, in the absence of evidence, how do we know that the cultural and political rule of the planters was the result of their dominance—that is, their hegemony—and against the class interests of the nonslaveholders? To say that the acceptance of slavery and the culture that justified it measures the power of the planter class because their class view was accepted by those who lacked the interest is to assume what one seeks to prove. The argument still rests on the assumption that the class interests of the two groups were different. In order to test the validity of hegemony as a historical fact and as an intellectual device for analytical purposes there must be some indication of what kind of evidence would disprove the hegemony of a ruling class in any given historical situation. To my knowledge no such evidence has been specified by those who support the idea of hegemony. In the absence of a test through potential disproof, the concept of hegemony becomes a tautology: All ruling classes exhibit hegemony over other classes for that is what a ruling class is by definition. Hegemony, in sum, does not *explain* how a class dominates a society; it merely describes, in a word rather than a phrase, that it is ruling.

Yet that is the question at issue. Was the Old South dominated by a self-conscious class that compelled or persuaded other social classes to its class position, or was it a society in which all strata of society were in substantial agreement in regard to basic social values, even though they might also be in conflict over some immediate economic interests? The assumption behind the idea of hegemony is that the relations between people and the means of production determine their class interests. Or as Genovese once wrote, "The confusion between Marxism and economic determinism arises from the Marxian definition of classes as groups, the members of which stand in a particular relationship to the means of production."[9] It is true that he goes on to say that the relationship to the means of production is only the beginning of the difference between classes and that these other historical differences need to be examined and studied for each class and for each society. Yet the basic antagonism between classes, originating in the differences in their relationship to the means of production, is never doubted. My contention is that such a conception of fundamental antagonism is an assumption that can be accepted only when it is established by historical evidence. Conflicting class interests cannot be assumed; they need to be determined and established through an examination of the sources. And that, I submit, has not been

9. Genovese, *In Red and Black*, 323.

done by those who espouse the idea of hegemony and class analysis of the history of the Old South.

Genovese does not use the phrase *false consciousness* in his analyses of the Old South, but some of his followers have. The term means that a subordinate social class might accept the values of a ruling class even though the subordinate class's interests and values were contrary to them; such a subjected class is said to exhibit "false consciousness." Analytically, the conception is merely another form of hegemony, for it imputes to past groups values and goals that historians today think those groups ought to have held despite the absence of evidence to that effect. For that reason, in my view, the conception of "false consciousness" is no more useful analytically than "hegemony."

The alternative to a class analysis is social consensus analysis. Basically, that analytical mode asserts, in regard to the antebellum South—and by extension to the South after the war as well—that on fundamental social values and goals the slaveholders and nonslaveholders were in agreement. This is not to say that there were no conflicts, political or otherwise in the antebellum South, for, of course, there were many. Men differed sharply over the extension of the franchise to propertyless white men, over the Bank of the United States, over the taxation of property in slaves, over the use of slaves as urban craftsmen, and over the counting of slaves as a basis for representation. Sometimes these and other differences were clearly between slaveholders and nonslaveholders. Yet they do not add up to a conflict between slaveholders and nonslaveholders over the fundamental values of an admittedly slave society. This is the precise issue disputed by those who advocate a class analysis, introducing the conception of hegemony, and those of us who press a social consensus interpretation, rejecting the idea of hegemony. It is my argument, in short, that nonslaveholders not only accepted slavery as a means of control over labor and over black people, but also aspired to become slaveholders themselves and to perpetuate the world slavery had made. That is but another way of saying that the interests of the slaveholders and the nonslaveholders were congruent, not antagonistic.[10]

Certainly the yeoman farmers' desire to acquire slaves has been shown by a variety of studies. The work of the Owsley school of social historians—notably that of Herbert Weaver, Blanche Clark, and Frank Owsley himself—has documented through the analysis of the manuscript census, the accumulation of slaves by erstwhile yeoman during the 1850s. Records of individuals and families alike attest to the widely held conviction that the acquisition of slaves and land was the surest way to financial success.

It has often been said that "only" a quarter of white families in the antebellum South owned slaves, implying a rather narrow social base for any popular connection to the peculiar institution. A better way of considering the matter, however, is to recognize that slave ownership was much more widely dispersed throughout southern society than the own-

10. Those readers who are close followers of Eugene Genovese's writings on hegemony might think that I have not given adequate attention in this regard to his recent essay "Yeoman Farmers in a Slaveholder's Democracy," *Agricultural History*, XLIX (April, 1975). In that essay Genovese seems to come close to the argument I have been making about the way one ought to test hegemony. And for good measure he castigates there those who would imply that the yeoman farmers were under the ideological, or any other, thumb of the planter class. I must confess that when I read that essay, I thought Genovese had indeed repudiated his earlier views. But as we have seen, Genovese's interpretations have never been static. His previous interpretation has had wide dissemination and wide acceptance among historians. And because that widely held interpretation is the one I wish to contest, rather than Genovese's most recent statement of it, I have not attempted to reconcile his apparent conception of hegemony in the recent essay on yeomanry with those that have gone before.

ership of an equivalent amount of stocks and securities in 1949. Otto Olsen has calculated that about 2 percent of United States families in 1949 owned $5,000 worth of securities, which was about equal to what a slave would have cost in 1860 if expressed in the twentieth-century value of money. Or, as he points out in another comparison, fewer than 10 percent of families in 1940 were headed by an employer of at least one worker, while in 1860 about 25 percent of southern families owned at least one slave.[11] In short, when the owner-ship of slaves is put into a comparative dimension, it becomes evident that slavery was not an interest of a favored few, but one so widely based that it can hardly be seen as an inevitable source of antagonism between a tiny ruling class and the rest of society. Many more southerners had a direct interest in slavery than twentieth-century Americans had in the owner-ship of stocks or in the hiring of workers. When this relatively widespread ownership of slaves is put in the context of an ex-panding economy, it is not difficult to understand why there was little or no fundamental conflict between those who al-ready owned slaves and those who did not. It was quite reasonable for a nonslaveholder to believe that his or her chances to acquire that kind of property were good.

That a slave society was popularly accepted in the South can be demonstrated in politics, too. Although virtually every southern state by 1850 permitted white men to vote without property qualifications, no significant movement arose to end slavery, as had occurred in the northern states between 1780 and 1800. For those who posit a fundamental antagonism be-tween slaveholders and nonslaveholders, this absence of a broad, popular movement against slavery in the South can only present problems. Generally, the explanations have been

11. Otto Olsen, "Historians and the Extent of Slave Ownership in the Southern United States," *Civil War History*, XVIII (June, 1972), 101–16.

two. The first is that the attacks on slavery and on the South from outside the region, especially after 1830 and the rise of abolitionism, killed off any indigenous southern antislavery movement because such a movement would have been perceived as a betrayal of the region. That explanation, of course, concedes the point that I wish to make here, for it rests on the assumption that most white southerners already accepted slavery as an integral and identifying institution of the region.

The second explanation for the absence of a southern antislavery movement is that the political system did not permit southern voters a choice in the matter, that no political party or organization was prepared to raise the issue; hence, the ordinary citizen or nonslaveholder had no way of expressing his hostility toward the slave system. This argument in effect is a special case of the hegemony argument. It is called into question, however, when we recall that in 1849 Kentucky did have a statewide election on the issue of emancipation. That year some southern antislavery leaders, among them Cassius M. Clay, introduced a plan for gradual emancipation, which was to be debated at the upcoming constitutional convention in Kentucky. Candidates for delegates to that convention ran on a platform of opposition to slavery. Nor were the opponents of slavery merely eccentrics or political figures of fun. Among them was not only the well known and highly respected Cassius M. Clay himself, but the even better known senior senator from the state, Henry Clay. Moreover, if slavery were ended in Kentucky, that eventuality would not threaten white supremacy since slaves constituted only a fifth of the population. Thus, nonslaveholding voters were confronted with as free a choice as possible in a society in which a major institution was being put to the test of popular opinion. Their response to that choice may thus reasonably be taken as an expression of their conception of their self-interest, not to be written off as merely a consequence of the so-called hegemony of the planting class. When the election of delegates was over, no more than 10,000 Kentuckians had voted for the antislavery delegates, even though the nonslaveholders—that is, those who presumably had little direct interest in the institution—outnumbered slaveholders by twenty to one. Cassius Clay later spoke out against slavery and for the nonslaveholders in his campaign for governor; but his final vote was less than 3,500, even though he had campaigned in some eighty counties— and, incidentally, without molestation. Thus, when offered a chance to put slavery on the way to extinction in Kentucky, nonslaveholders as a class refused.

Ironically enough, those who seek evidence of class hostility toward the slave system find it principally in the writings of large planters. Apparently, the planters, like some modern historians, thought the nonslaveholders ought to have felt envy or resentment over slavery. Daniel Hamilton of South Carolina wrote a friend in February, 1860, "I mistrust our own people more than I fear all of the efforts of the abolitionists." [12] And at least one historian has argued that a large part of the corpus of proslavery literature written by southerners was actually directed at the nonslaveholders in the South, those who. were thought to be potentially, if not actually, hostile to the slave regime. In a system of political equality for all white males, perhaps that fear was reasonable. Yet without the corroboration of actual hostility on a wide scale by nonslaveholders against the slave regime, the fears of the planters can no more establish the existence of class hostility toward slavery than their equally well-documented fear of slave insurrections can establish the widespread existence of slave conspiracies. All that the planters' fears about the loyalty of the

12. Quoted in Steven A. Channing, *Crisis of Fear: Secession in South Carolina* (New York: Simon & Schuster, 1970), 256.

nonslaveholders show is the insecurity they felt about holding that property. The fear of white disloyalty would seem
to bespeak more guilt among slaveholders than hostility by
nonslaveholders toward slavery and the society it had
created.

All of these pieces of evidence for believing that the ordinary white southerner accepted the slave society because it
was consistent with his or her own interests have been dis-
missed by those who talk of planter hegemony and class
conflict in the Old South. The heart of that argument, to cite
Genovese again, has been that the "success of a ruling class in
establishing its hegemony depends entirely on its ability to
convince the lower classes that its interest are those of society
at large—that it defends the common sensibility and stands
for a natural and proper social order." [13] What we have not
been told by proponents of hegemony is how we know it was
the planting class's hegemony that accounted for the identification of interest rather than *the actual self-interest* of the
nonslaveholders. To someone who does not accept hegemony
as an explanation, it seems quite plausible that the interests of
nonslaveholders and planters, as each defines them for himself, are at least parallel, not antagonistic. In fact, that is my
reading of the nature of social relations in the Old South. Yet,
as pointed out earlier, the underlying assumption of the
hegemony argument is that those who own the means of production and those who do not must have divergent and ulti-
mately antagonistic outlooks. Again, it seems to me that
hegemony assumes a social division that must be proved
through the analysis of historical evidence. Whether the
nonslaveholders and planters actually were divided and antagonistic is certainly a pertinent question to ask about the an-

13. Genovese, *In Red and Black*, 407.

tebellum South. But the answer must not be *assumed*, as I think the conception of planter hegemony and class conflict does. For in assuming it, an examination of the pertinent historical evidence is rendered either unnecessary or irrelevant.

A more convincing approach, it seems to me, is one in which the self-interest of a social group is ascertained either from direct verbal expressions or inferred from behavior. In that way no assumption is made that when two or more social or economic groups or classes exist they must always be antagonistic (or always harmonious, for that matter). With such an approach, the available evidence can be used to ascertain whether socioeconomic groups were in fact antagonistic or whether they found they were in essential agreement. At no time, of course, does this approach deny the existence of social classes—defined as groups with different amounts of resources—or deny conflict between such groups. The question at issue is whether these different groups were self-conscious about their identity and whether they exhibited antagonism over fundamental social values and goals. When this approach is followed, the antebellum South is quite understandable as a society in which the overwhelming majority of white southerners accepted slavery and the values that surrounded it, because that kind of society served their interests as well as those of the slaveholders. And one reason it did serve their interests is that the majority of the southern people helped to shape that society; it was not simply the product of a dominant, slaveholding class, as Genovese argues.

High on the lists of those interests were the economic gains that nonslaveholders anticipated from one day holding slaves themselves, as well as the gains they received because blacks were kept under control and denominated as socially inferior to whites. This latter explanation for the acceptance of a slave society by nonslaveholders does not usually come under the heading of material gains or self-interest, but human beings have psychological as well as material interests. In a society that puts a premium upon mobility and individual achievement it was not an insignificant gain for a white person to know that blacks, as slaves and free people, were kept in an inferior social position. Such a social hierarchical arrangement brought not only economic advantages, but social and psychological status as well.

A further reason for doubting the class interpretation of the antebellum South, as Genovese defines that interpretation, is suggested by the large number of slaveholders among the opponents of slavery in the South. This is true of people like Angelina and Sarah Grimké of South Carolina and James Birney of Alabama, who left the South in order to become active abolitionists, and many who remained in the slave states. I do not want to make too much of the opposition to slavery in the South, for clearly most white southerners were not hostile to the institution. Yet the handful of southern antislavery advocates who remained in the South, whether as colonizationists or as outright opponents of human bondage, turn out almost always to be from the slaveholding class or to have been slaveholders of consequence at one time. Among such people were Henry Clay, Cassius Clay, Robert Breckinridge, Mary Minor Blackford, Henry Ruffner, and William Gaston. Among them would also be included about half of the fifty-eight men in the Virginia House of Delegates in 1832 who voted to have the legislature move ahead toward eventual emancipation. Their numbers are not significant in comparison with those who supported slavery or remained silent on the subject. But among those southerners who opposed the institution at all, it is striking that slaveholders were the most numerous. Hinton Rowan Helper's The Impending Crisis of the South, published in 1857, made a great impact on northern public opinion because it was an antislavery tract written by a nonslaveholding southern white. But among southern antislavery writers, Hinton Helper's humble social origins were conspicuous for their rarity.

Slaveholders divided more significantly over secession, the supposed solution to the slaveholders' fear of outside interference with their social order. William L. Barney's study of secession in Mississippi and Alabama, Ralph Wooster's dissection of the secession conventions, and Michael Johnson's book on secession in Georgia all document the diverse and often contradictory positions taken by the slaveholding elite about the merits of secession. In Georgia, for example, voters for the secessionist and cooperationist causes were divided about equally, with planters well represented in both camps. The town counties in Georgia, moreover, were the strongest for secession, though one would have expected rural planters to be the most favorably disposed in that direction.[14]

One reason that slaveholders were not united on secession was that it was not at all clear that leaving the Union was the best way to protect slavery—a central concern of most southerners. As John S. Carlile, a slaveholder and an admitted believer in the morality of slavery asked his colleagues at the Virginia convention in 1861, "How long, if you were to dissolve this Union would African slavery have a foothold in this portion of the land? I venture the assertion that it would not exist in Virginia five years after separation, and nowhere in the Southern states twenty years after," he predicted. "How could it maintain itself, with the whole civilized world, backed by what they call their international law, arrayed for its ultimate extinction?" On the other hand, he continued,

14. Michael P. Johnson, *Toward a Patriarchal Republic: The Secession of Georgia* (Baton Rouge: Louisiana State University Press, 1977).

within the Union there were all kinds of constitutional, not to mention popular, protections for the South's peculiar institution.[15]

Those who, like Carlile, thought secession an unpromising way to preserve slavery proved quite correct. Within five years of the decision to leave the Union, slavery was dead not only within Virginia as Carlile had presciently said, but in the whole South. How the South reacted to that sudden end to slavery also casts light on the nature of antebellum society and the continuity of southern history. But that matter I will leave for further discussion later. Right now I would like to examine the second part of Genovese's interpretation of the Old South.

Even if one rejects Genovese's contention that the antebellum South was shaped by a self-conscious planter class, that conclusion does not invalidate the proposition that the Old South exhibited a different world view from that of the rest of the country. C. Vann Woodward, for example, who does not describe himself as a Marxist, nevertheless has advanced a conception of the South's culture very similar to, if not identical with, Genovese's. Woodward has called the antebellum South, it will be remembered, not only a slave society, but one that "had grown up and miraculously flourished in the heart of a thoroughly bourgeois and partly puritanical republic" and "had renounced its bourgeois origins and elaborated and painfully rationalized its institutional, legal, metaphysical, and religious defenses." It is to this assertion that the slave South developed a different world view from the rest of the United States that I now turn.

One way of approaching the question is through the intellectual history of the South. In supporting his argument that

15. George H. Reese (ed.), *Proceedings of the Virginia State Convention of 1861* (4 vols.; Richmond: Virginia State Library, 1965), III, 169.

the South developed a world view deeply divergent from that of the rest of the nation, Eugene Genovese has identified George Fitzhugh of Virginia as the ideologue of the planter class, the man who best expressed the outlook and the implications of a prebourgeois slave society. And it is true that out of an examination of George Fitzhugh's works emerges a conception of a society, of the place of the individual, and of slavery itself that is quite at variance with the dominant values of the United States as a whole. As Louis Hartz pointed out in *The Liberal Tradition in America*, only in the thought of a few people in the antebellum South, notably that of George Fitzhugh, has a truly conservative political philosophy been evident in the whole range of American political thought. All others have been variants of the liberal persuasion descended from John Locke and Adam Smith.

An emphasis upon the thought of Fitzhugh can only seem strange to anyone conversant with the political and intellectual history of the Old South. For, as Genovese himself candidly admits, Fitzhugh carried little of the intellectual weight and exercised none of the political influence of, say, John C. Calhoun, or, for that matter, of half a dozen other leading southern spokesmen. Given Genovese's conception of the South, however, the trouble with Calhoun is that his political ideas, even in a slave society, show that the South espoused the same world view as the rest of liberal America.

It is quite true that Calhoun has often been taken as a conservative if only because he defended slavery. In that sense of conservative—one who seeks to preserve the status quo— Calhoun is clearly not a reformer or a nineteenth-century liberal. And he certainly repudiated much of the Jeffersonian heritage when he rejected the idea of natural rights from which so much of Jeffersonian liberalism derived. But then in the twentieth century, most liberals have also abandoned the concept of natural rights without losing their credentials as liberals. In the sense that Louis Hartz taught us to think about conservatism, Calhoun is clearly a part of the liberal tradition that is the centerpiece of American political thought. Calhoun may have found certain aspects of political democracy dangerous, but he never doubted that reason and individualism were at the heart of the good society. One need only look at his solution to the question of how to preserve slavery to recognize how much a child of Locke and the Enlightenment Calhoun was, as compared to Fitzhugh. Calhoun's device of the concurrent majority and his defense of it in his *Disquisition on Government* are quite contrary to Fitzhugh's or Edmund Burke's emphasis upon the organic nature of society. What Calhoun argued for was the establishment of a brand new institution in American government to meet a social need. Men would sit down and, through the application of their reason, would arrive at a solution to the social and political problems that confronted them. Having arrived at a solution, they would then adjust their governmental structure to accommodate that solution. Such a rationalistic approach to government and society was precisely the objection that Burke and other European conservatives had raised against the French Revolution. Calhoun's approach to the reordering of society and government through the use of reason was quite within the liberal and Enlightenment tradition that had produced the state and federal constitutions after the American Revolution, and which called for their periodic renovation in the same rational fashion.

The idea of the concurrent majority, as Calhoun set it forth, required the application of reason in politics and the recognition of individual self-interest, just as any liberal would have advocated. The mechanism of the concurrent majority is that a minority of states could prevent the decision of a majority of states from going into effect. When opponents of the idea pointed out that the operations of the government would be paralyzed by such a veto power in the hands of a minority, Calhoun, in true Enlightenment fashion, responded by denying that paralysis would result. The majority, he said, would recognize the just claims of the minority and accommodation would ensue. That is, men in conflict would be reasonable. Calhoun certainly had the same interest as Fitzhugh in seeking to protect slavery; but unlike Fitzhugh, Calhoun significantly chose a solution based on reason, that is, a liberal means to that end. And that is why Louis Hartz refers to Calhoun as a representative of the Reactionary Enlightenment.

Within the context of the antebellum years the more representative southerner was clearly Calhoun, not Fitzhugh. Calhoun, after all, accepted states' rights, a strict construction of the Constitution, and the perpetuation of an agricultural society—the well-known hallmarks of antebellum southern politicians. Fitzhugh, on the other hand, had little use for states' rights or strict construction. "With inexorable sequence," he wrote in his *Cannibals All!* "Let Alone is made to usher in No-Government. North and South our [conservatives'] danger is the same, and our remedies, though differing in degree, must in character be the same. Let Alone must be repudiated," he concluded, referring to laissez-faire doctrine, "if we would have any government. We must, in all sections, act upon the principle that the world is 'too little governed.'" In the same book, he spelled out his basic disagreement with virtually all southern politicians of his time. "Government is the life of a nation, and as no one can foresee the various future circumstances of social, any more than of individual life, it is absurd to define on paper, at the birth of either the nation or individual, what they shall do and what not do." So much for the idea of a written constitution or the protection of minority rights through the device of the concurrent majority. "Broad construction of constitutions," he asserted, is preferred over strict construction because it "is as good as no constitution, for it leaves the nation to adapt itself to circumstances, but strict construction will destroy any nation, for action is necessary to national conservation, and constitution-makers cannot foresee what action will be necessary. . . . A constitution, strictly construed, is absolutely inconsistent with permanent national existence."[16] Fitzhugh may have provided in his writings what the planter class of the South *ought* to have espoused in order to defend slavery and the society built around it, as Genovese has argued, but clearly it was not the outlook that the leaders of the South *did* espouse.

The value to us today of Fitzhugh as a southern thinker is that by an examination of his ideas we learn the limits of southern differences from the rest of the United States. He provides a revealing measure of the extent to which the antebellum South espoused a different world view from that of the rest of the country. For if Fitzhugh's ideas were well suited to a prebourgeois slave society, then the failure of articulate southerners to follow his ideas shows that they had in fact not departed from the bourgeois, liberal values against which Fitzhugh raised his voice so powerfully but also so ineffectively. Indeed, when the divergence between Fitzhugh's ideas on government and politics and those of the vast majority of southern planters who followed Calhoun is recognized, it is clear that the only reason Fitzhugh received any hearing in the South is because he provided yet another defense of

16. George Fitzhugh, *Cannibals All! or Slaves without Masters*, ed. C. Vann Woodward (Cambridge: Belknap Press of Harvard University Press, 1960), 247, 249.

slavery. Apparently, southerners would accept any defense of slavery, even when it came from someone so out of intellectual tune with his fellow southerners.

If Fitzhugh fails to qualify as a representative southerner and thus cannot provide support for the assertion that the planters' world view diverged from that of the North, there were other southerners who *were* representative of southern political thought, but whose values were quite in agreement with those of other Americans. This congruence in values is especially evident in the proslavery arguments. The defense of slavery as it was elaborated in the middle of the nineteenth century was primarily—though not exclusively—a southern product. And to that extent the South was set apart from the rest of the nation. Some southerners, however, went beyond a mere defense of slavery. They advanced the proposition that slavery was justified because Negroes were biologically inferior to whites. It is true that some southerners, like Henry Clay, refused publicly to accept the argument that slavery was a positive good. But the issue is not whether all southerners defended slavery on biological grounds, but simply that a significant number of southerners did. The point I wish to make is that in this respect the South was unique. No other society in the New World in which Negro slavery was established found it necessary to defend slavery on racial grounds to the extent that the American South did. All slave societies, ancient and modern, defended slavery—usually on the grounds that slaves were property and their labor was essential to the economy. But only in the antebellum South were defenses also erected on the assumption that blacks were natural slaves or racially inferior to whites.

At the same time that a biological defense of slavery set the South apart from other slave societies, it also revealed how close in values the South was to the rest of the United

States. For only if the South had *not* found it necessary to defend slavery on grounds of race would it have shown itself to have a different value system from the North. The reason the other slave societies of the New World did not find it necessary to arrive at a racial defense of slavery is that they saw no fundamental contradiction between slavery and the social order. In those slave societies slavery was only one of several forms of subordination, albeit a severe one. In the United States, on the other hand, with its historic emphasis upon equality and freedom, slavery was an anomaly. It denied by its existence the principles of the Declaration of Independence and the long history of political democracy that had gradually removed all qualifications for political participation except manhood. There was no place in American political thought for degrees of freedom and equality; *all* men are created equal, the Declaration had said. Slavery could not be defended on the ground that some men were deserving of more freedom than others. But if it could be argued that some persons were not truly men, that they were biologically inferior to white men, then slavery acquired a new and surer defense in the American context of equality. And so America became the one slave society in which race became an important defense of slavery.

At the time, southern defenders of slavery made quite clear that they accepted the political values of other Americans, for they sought to realize them. Many years ago Fletcher Green demonstrated that the antebellum South participated fully in the development of democratic political institutions. The movement for the abandonment of property qualifications for voting and officeholding, as well as other democratic political reforms, achieved as much success in the southern as in the northern states. The political equality of white men was as much an article of faith in the South as in the North. "In the

South," said Mississippi fire-eater Albert Gallatin Brown, "all men are equal. I mean of course white men; negroes are not men within the meaning of the Declaration." Or as Henry Wise of Virginia put it, "Break down slavery and you would with the same blow destroy the great democratic principle of equality among men." Thomas R. R. Cobb of Georgia also testified to the agreement between southerners and northerners on the equality of white men. "It matters not that [the white voter] is no slaveholder; he is not of the inferior race; he is a free-born citizen; he engages in no menial occupation. The poorest meets the richest as an equal; sits at his table with him; salutes him as a neighbor; meets him in every public assembly and stands on the same social platform." [17]

At the same time, the exclusion of blacks from the meaning of "men within the Declaration," as Brown phrased it, was quite consistent with northern conceptions of political democracy. In 1860 only six states of the North permitted blacks to vote, and free Negroes were not permitted to migrate into some of the middle western states. In all the states of the North, blacks were subjected to social and economic discrimination. As Leon Litwack has shown at length in *North of Slavery*, blacks were second-class citizens, even though free, in all of the northern states. In both sections the meaning of political democracy was the same: only white men participated equally in the voting booth and the statehouse. Despite the myth of aristocratic southern politics, no southern politician, no matter how many slaves he owned, any more than

17. The quotation from Brown appears in Charles Sellers (ed.), *The Southerner as American* (New York: E. P. Dutton, 1964), 64; the statement from Wise is quoted in George M. Fredrickson, *The Black Image in the White Mind: The Debate on Afro-American Character and Destiny, 1817–1914* (New York: Harper and Row, 1971), 62; the remark by Cobb is from Thomas R. R. Cobb, *An Inquiry into the Law of Negro Slavery in the United States of America. . . .* (Reprint of 1858 ed.; New York: Negro Universities Press, 1968), ccxiii.

any northern politician, no matter how many workers he employed, dared to speak publicly against white manhood suffrage. In that sense, the people ruled in both sections.

In regard to other social values, southerners were also in agreement with northerners. The ideal of social mobility and competitive independence, which Eric Foner discerned at the root of the ideology of the Republican party of the North, was also evident south of the Mason-Dixon Line. Quite properly Foner points to the westward movement as at once a measure and a sign of the northern belief in mobility and economic and social striving for individual improvement. The South, too, of course, participated in that same westward movement and for the very same reasons. Most of the southerners who made that westward trek—filling up Tennessee, Alabama, Mississippi, Louisiana, Arkansas, and Texas—were not slaveholders, though many of them became so in time. They demonstrated the same concern for geographical and social mobility and advancement that characterized other Americans. Certainly the studies of the Owsley school of southern social historians reveal many examples of social mobility in the rural South, which are much like those detailed for the rural Northwest. The South, after all, like the North during these years, as economic historians have recently shown, was an expanding and prosperous economy. Owsley's finding that some 80 percent of farmers in the South owned the land they farmed reveals, too, that the individualistic independence of most white southerners was firmly grounded in property ownership, just as Jefferson and the American liberal tradition said it ought to be. Eugene Genovese himself has recently paid deserved tribute to those fiercely individualistic southern yeomen. "Slavery, it has long been asserted, had numbed the lower-class whites quite as much as it had ostensibly numbed the enslaved blacks," he writes. "Southern abolitionists, for understandable reasons, became the bitterest proponents of this argument and railed in frustration at the non-slaveholders' groveling before the aristocratic pretensions of the haughty planters. Yet we know very well that those non-slaveholders were touchy, proud people who hardly specialized in groveling and who were as quick as the planters to shed blood over questions of honor. We know also that they seized and maintained substantial political rights and were largely responsible for some of the most democratic state constitutions in the United States." [18] In summary, save for the southern defense of slavery, it is difficult to find political or social values that were dominant in the North that were not also widely present and deeply held in the South.

The endurance and flourishing of slavery in the South long after it had been set on the path to extinction in the North undoubtedly produced a different society in the South, one that made the region distinctive. But that distinctiveness did not add up to a different world view or make the society pre-bourgeois in thought or action. On the contrary, I would argue that the recourse to a racial defense of slavery on the part of the South was a response to the fear that the American—and therefore, the southern—value of freedom and equality would be extended first to slaves and then to blacks. Today we recognize that the fear was unfounded. The Republican party may have opposed slavery, but only in the territories; it raised no direct objections to slavery in the South. And Lincoln and his party were even prepared, on the eve of the Civil War, to trade the perpetual protection of slavery where it already existed, for a prohibition against its extension into the territories where it did not exist. We also know that even when the Republicans did end slavery, their position on equality be-

18. Eugene D. Genovese, "Yeoman Farmers in a Slaveholder's Democracy," *Agricultural History*, XLIX (April, 1975), 331.

tween blacks and whites was only weakly held. At the time, however, these limits to Republican antislavery and egalitarian principles were not recognized by most southerners. As often happens in moments of historical crisis, southerners mistook a difference in degree between themselves and the dominant group in the North for a difference in kind. Certainly, a difference over the future of slavery was a sharp difference in values, but it did not reshape the whole constellation of values that northerners and southerners held in common. David Potter has gone so far as to find more agreement between northerners and southerners at that time than a century later.

Most Northerners and most Southerners were farmer folk who cultivated their own land and cherished a fierce devotion to the principles of personal independence and social equalitarianism. They shared a great pride in the Revolutionary heritage, the Constitution and "republican institutions," and an ignorance about Europe, which they regarded as decadent and infinitely inferior to the United States. They also shared a somewhat intolerant, orthodox Protestantism, a faith in rural virtues, and a commitment to the gospel of hard work, acquisition and success.[19]

It is relevant in this connection, too, that those southerners who were most interested in establishing a separate South— that is, a Confederate South—were usually among those most vigorous in advancing the racial defense of slavery. Less self-conscious southerners, like Henry Clay who repudiated the positive-good theory of slavery, were less sure that blacks were racially inferior. That difference between two kinds of southern leaders is revealing. It suggests that even those who might be thought to differ most in their world views from northerners—because they argued for slavery and secession

19. David M. Potter, The Impending Crisis, 1848–1861 (New York: Harper and Row, 1976), 472.

so ardently—nevertheless still accepted the American value of equality. For they felt compelled to erect a defense of slavery that assumed these values among the southern people. Those who point to Fitzhugh's defense of slavery as eschewing racial prejudice emphasize that he couched his argument in class terms. Fitzhugh's point was that all societies subordinate the working class, whatever its color or race; slavery, he said, was only a more severe form of subordination. Slavery did not differ in kind, Fitzhugh contended, from the subordination of the white working class in the North, except that it might be more benign in its impact. Those historians, like Genovese, who point to Fitzhugh to show that racism was not at the root of the planters' ideology once again ignore the atypical character of Fitzhugh in the intellectual history of the antebellum South. Whatever may have been Fitzhugh's personal success in avoiding race as a justification or defense of slavery, few of the southern apologists for the peculiar institution were able to follow him. And the reason they could not was simply that as Americans they could not advance class distinctions as a justification for subordination, for to do so would have violated American conceptions of equality and freedom for white men. Significantly, a class defense of slavery, such as Fitzhugh sought to erect, could no more appeal to southerners than it could to northerners, because both drew upon the same American values. The point is neatly clinched when it is recognized that in the end, in April, 1861, even George Fitzhugh accepted a racial defense of slavery, acknowledging thereby that in America an appeal to hierarchy or class subordination alone could not protect the institution of human bondage.[20]

If, on the eve of the Civil War, North and South did not

20. See the trenchant analysis of Fitzhugh's thought and its limitations in Fredrickson, *The Black Image in the White Mind*, 56–70.

have different world views, they were nevertheless different societies. Indeed, just because of those differences, which clustered around the existence of slavery in the South, eleven southern states broke away to form the Confederate States of America. The way that break took place, however, ought to give us still further pause in accepting the argument that the differences between the North and South were so deep and so divergent as to be called differences in world view. It is true that the rapidity with which the seven states of the Deep South seceded can be interpreted as a measure of the deep differences between the sections. Within the seven weeks between December 20, 1860, and February 7, 1861, all seven of the states had voted to leave the Union and formed the Confederate States of America. That alacrity, however, has a different look when examined more closely. The secessionists were so unsure of the popular support for their cause that they felt it imperative to move rapidly before the shock and alleged threat of Lincoln's election in November, 1860, receded from the minds of southerners. As one secessionist in South Carolina wrote privately, "I do not believe that the common people understand. In fact, I know that they do not understand it; but whoever waited for the common people when a great move was to be made? We must make the move and force them to follow."[21] This lack of confidence that the people would sustain them also underlies the refusal of the first six of the seceding states to hold popular referenda on the decision to secede. Only Texas, which was the last of the seven states of the Deep South to secede, held a referendum. By then, however, it was not only clear that secession was a fact; but for Texas, given its geographical location, it was a near necessity. Even with all that haste, the elections to the

21. Quoted in David M. Potter, *Lincoln and His Party in the Secession Crisis* (New Haven: Yale University Press, 1942), 208.

secession conventions to several of the Deep South states had been uncomfortably close. In Georgia, for example, the vote was 44,142 to 41,632, and that is the most generous estimate of secession sentiment in a count that is in dispute. In Louisiana the secessionists prevailed only by 20,214 to 18,451.

Outside the Deep South not even the election of Lincoln or the creation of the Confederacy was sufficient to move the other slave states out of the Union. In fact, in Tennessee and North Carolina the voters resoundingly turned down a call to hold a convention at all, thus preventing any immediate move to join the newly established Confederacy. Arkansas and Virginia did hold conventions, but neither of them was prepared to vote for secession. The Arkansas convention instead voted against secession and then adjourned in March, 1861. The Virginia convention remained in session, but voted neither for nor against secession. Only with the firing on Fort Sumter and the opening of the military phase of secession were the four states of the upper South moved to forsake the Union their fathers had helped to found. As David Potter has concluded, secession was probably not the will of the southern people, not even those in the Deep South.

Finally, the character of the South after the Civil War shows in another way that the ending of slavery did not mark a major break in the continuity of southern history, any more than the existence of slavery had created a separate nation and a different world view within the southern part of the United States. The persistence of the South's distinctiveness, even after slavery was gone, is the subject we turn to now.

IV   The Persistence
of Southern Distinctiveness

UNDOUBTEDLY, the most persuasive single piece of evidence that antebellum southerners had developed a different world view from that of other Americans is the secession of eleven southern states and the formation of the Confederacy. Certainly no other region of the nation ever felt so alienated as to take such a radical step, though New England at one time came close. Yet, as many historians have pointed out, what is striking about the Confederacy is how congruent its institutions and political values were with those of the United States. One searches in vain through the Confederate Constitution, for example, for those innovations and changes that would signal the arrival on the world stage of a slave-holders' republic, which repudiated the bourgeois elements characterizing the United States. All the protections of private property, business enterprise, and the rights of individuals contained in the United States Constitution were retained in the Confederate Constitution. Only in limiting the president to a single term of six years and its prescription that the Post Office pay its own way does the Confederate Constitution deviate from the United States Constitution in a mildly innovative way. There are protections for slavery, to be sure, but they are not nearly as strong as one might anticipate. For example, free states were not to be excluded from the new Confederacy. Even the right of secession is left unstated. It is true that "Al-

mighty God" is invoked in the preamble, whereas the deity
never appears in the United States Constitution. But that addi-
tion is not as signifficant as it might seem when we recollect
how often Abraham Lincoln, that epitome of the bourgeois
North, made references to God in state papers. The Confederate Constitution, in short, makes evident how conservative
southerners were, but only in the conventional sense of
minimizing or containing change, rather than in the Burkean
or Hartzian sense of abandoning the American liberal tradition.

Nowhere is this point more clearly recognized than in the
frequently heard argument by southerners that secession was
justified by the experience of Americans in 1776. On both
occasions—in 1776 and 1860—southerners emphasized, the
resort to radical measures was dictated by the violations of
ancient rights by those in power. As one Georgian wrote,
southerners should "do as Washington, Hancock, and other
conservative Americans did, when coercive measures were
adopted by the King and Parliament to collect three pence tax
on tea imported into Boston—join the resisting party and aid
in achieving perfect independence."[1] Those southerners who
justified secession frequently saw themselves and their region
following in the footsteps of their Revolutionary forefathers.
Southerners, wrote one Georgia woman, just wanted to be "let
alone. . . . The idea is preposterous," she went on, that northerners "a people like ourselves whose republican independence was won by a rebellion, whose liberty [was] achieved
by secession . . . should attempt to coerce us"[2] One southern

1. Quoted in Michael P. Johnson, *Toward a Patriarchal Republic: The
Secession of Georgia* (Baton Rouge: Louisiana State University Press, 1977).

2. Quoted in James L. Roark, "Masters without Slaves: Southern Planters in the Civil War and Reconstruction," (Ph.D. dissertation, Stanford
University, 1973), 18. Roark's dissertation will be published early in 1977
by W. W. Norton.

newspaper, apparently to underscore the comparison between 1776 and 1861, reprinted in full Patrick Henry's "Give
Me Liberty or Give Me Death" speech. Even those southerners
who were ready to abandon the Union were still drawing
upon those bourgeois political principles that all Americans
adhered to, among which was the liberal principle of the right
of revolution.

The comparison between the South's course in 1861 and
the secession of the American colonies from the British Em-
pire some ninety years earlier has a significance beyond the
historical justification to which southerners put it. It also provides us with a fresh historical example of how two peoples
might be sufficiently different for one to seek political independence from the other and yet not hold different world
views. For as Bernard Bailyn, Gordon Wood, and other historians of the American Revolutionary era have shown, the origins of the rhetoric and political philosophy of 1776 were
clearly British. And even Eugene Genovese, I think, would see
America and Britain as having the same world view in 1776.
Yet if the British and Americans shared a common world
view at the time of the Revolution, their respective societies
certainly differed, just as the social character of North and
South differed in 1860.

Indeed, the very defeat of the Confederacy is a succinct
and striking measure of how different northern and southern
societies had become as a result of slavery. Running through
the conventional explanations for the South's defeat, one is
always struck by the fact that each of the reasons can be traced
back to the kind of society the South had become as a result of
slavery. If, for example, the defeat is blamed on the South's
lack of manufacturing capability, on its failure to develop an
industrial base for modern war, then the commitment to agriculture that slavery fostered certainly is an important part of

the explanation for defeat. Moreover, the South's emphasis upon cotton fostered just the kind of economy that could only lose in a war in which the enemy controlled the sea on which arrived the internal needs of the region's unbalanced economy. The North's diversified or balanced economy may have received some setbacks from the war, as recent economic historians have shown, but those were little more than interruptive slowdowns, not the absolute declines that the South sustained.

If, as Frank Owsley contended years ago, the South's lack of unity and the successful invoking of states' rights by leaders like Zebulon Vance, Alexander Stephens, and Joseph E. Brown were at the root of its defeat, then the elaborate defense of states' rights worked out during the antebellum years must bear a large share of the blame for the defeat. The principal reason southern political leaders and thinkers had pressed hard their defense of states' rights was to erect a barrier against a federal power that seemed to threaten slavery. Men and women trained through a lifetime of resisting centralized power in Washington in defense of slavery could not easily forget those lessons just because the central authority shifted 150 miles south to Richmond. Even a southern nationalist like Jefferson Davis found himself inhibited in using his full powers as president of the Confederacy because a lifetime of legalistic politics in defense of the South and slavery could not easily be sloughed off. Yet concern with legalities was clearly the wrong tactic when seeking to win a revolution. And if Robert E. Lee's weakness as a military commander lay in his unwillingness to look beyond Virginia, as T. Harry Williams and others have argued, then that historic, if quite understandable, emphasis upon states' right must be recognized as another way in which the Confederacy's defeat grew out of the antebellum South's defense of slavery.

Slavery had always been more than a molder of peculiarly southern attitudes and social development; it had also been a source of political and social division within the South. Many nonslaveholders fought for the Confederacy, to be sure. Indeed, since only a small minority of southerners owned slaves, the bulk of the armies of the South must have been made up of nonslaveholders. Yet the division of the South into slaveholding and nonslaveholding areas was an important source of discontent and defection within the Confederacy. Northern Alabama, east Tennessee, western North Carolina, north Georgia, and northwestern Arkansas, were only the largest and most familiar strongholds of southern resistance to the Confederacy. All of those I have listed, of course, were areas in which slavery was only weakly established. From these areas, too, came most of the 54,000 southern whites who joined the Union Army to help suppress the slaveholders' republic.

If one of the reasons the South was defeated was because it was unable to gain foreign recognition, then slavery played a part there, too. Although the presence of slavery in the South was not the prime reason the British failed to recognize the Confederacy, the persistence of slavery in the South after Lincoln made the Emancipation Proclamation insured that Britain would not thereafter recognize the Confederacy. Southern leaders themselves acknowledged the burden slavery placed upon their cause when, at the very end of the war, they offered emancipation in return for British recognition of the Confederacy.

If, as Eric McKitrick has suggested, the defeat of the Confederacy was in large part a consequence of the new country's lack of a strong, competitive two-party system, that explanation, too, can be traced to the Old South's defense of slavery. For almost twenty years, from the early 1830s on, the southern states had enjoyed a vigorous two-party system, with Whigs and Democrats contending. No state was safely Whiggish or Democratic, and between 1832 and 1852 neither party could be sure of winning the region as a whole. But that healthy political rivalry ended in the 1850s as the political defense of slavery, both nationally and regionally, intensified. As a result, the Confederacy emerged with only a single party, the Democratic. The Whig party, we now know, was underground—a strong memory in the minds of many voters, but without either visibility or organization. The North, on the other hand, profited from the rivalry between Democrats and Republicans, as McKitrick has imaginatively shown.[3] Lincoln, for example, could always count upon support for his policies and for the war effort from his fellow Republicans. Jefferson Davis, who had no party organization and no rival to the Democratic party to keep it alert, lacked that advantage.

If the defeat of the Confederacy stemmed from what David Donald has called an "excess of democracy," then a South molded by slavery contributed in another way to the downfall of the Confederacy. For what Donald means by an "excess of democracy" is not so much political democracy as individualism and lack of social discipline. And those aspects of life surely can be traced in a large degree to the agricultural nature of the antebellum South, with its enduring frontier, its widespread violence, its lack of urbanization. All of these we have traced back to slavery.

Finally, the very defeat of the Confederacy, whatever reasons one might assign for it, enhanced the distinctiveness of

3. Eric L. McKitrick, "Party Politics and the Urban and Confederate War Efforts," in William Nisbet Chambers and Walter Dean Burnham (eds.), *The American Party System: States of Political Development* (New York: Oxford University Press, 1967).

the South. As C. Vann Woodward has emphasized, no other Americans have experienced defeat in war so completely and so devastatingly. No other Americans have experienced directly an army of occupation. No other Americans, as they think about the Civil War, have that visceral reaction which William Faulkner so powerfully described in *Intruder in the Dust*:

For every Southern boy fourteen years old, not once but whenever he wants it, there is the instant when it's still not yet two o'clock on that July afternoon in 1863, the brigades are in position behind the rail fence, the guns are laid and ready in the woods . . . and Pickett himself with . . . his hat in one hand . . . and his sword in the other looking up the hill waiting for Longstreet to give the word and it's all in the balance, it hasn't happened yet, it hasn't even begun yet, it not only hasn't begun yet but there is still time for it not to begin against that position and those circumstances which made more men than Garnett and Kemper and Armstead and Wilcox look grave yet it's going to begin, we all know that, we have come too far with too much at stake and that moment doesn't need even a fourteen-year-old boy to think *This time. Maybe this time* with all this much to lose and all this much to gain: Pennsylvania, Maryland, the world, the golden dome of Washington itself to crown with desperate and unbelievable victory the desperate gamble, the cast made two years ago.[4]

Insofar as southerners lack some of that belief in progress or that optimistic outlook upon the future which is so characteristic of Americans, that lack is surely to be related to the remembrance that the South lost a war. Certainly the modern southern interest in the Confederacy, the war, its heroes, and its legend amply testify to the persistence of that memory. Indeed, David Potter has recently traced a "deeply felt southern nationalism" to "the shared sacrifices, the shared efforts, and the shared defeat (which is often more unifying than victory)

4. William Faulkner, *Intruder in the Dust* (New York: Random House, 1948), 194–95.

of the Civil War. The Civil War," he adds "did far more to produce a southern nationalism which flourished in the cult of the Lost Cause than southern nationalism did to produce the war."[5]

Yet if the defeat of the Confederacy has left a long legacy of emotion and rhetoric, the ending of slavery left few regrets upon the southern mind. Although historians are in almost total agreement today about the centrality of slavery to the coming of secession and the creation of the Confederacy, the abolition of slavery in 1865 brought almost no resistance from southerners and remarkably few regrets thereafter. Even a former slaveholder and Confederate like Alabama's Henry Hilliard could assure Brazilian abolitionists in 1880 that "fortunately for us in the United States, even the humane system of slavery which prevailed there has passed away forever. The shadow upon the dial of human conscience," he went on, "must go back many degrees before any considerable number of men in the Southern States of the Union would consent to see slavery restored."[6]

For our purposes here, this clean ending of slavery has an important implication. It is true that some southerners found a slave society so congenial or indispensable that they could not contemplate a world in which the slave plantation was no more. Some of these people emigrated to Mexico, Cuba, and Brazil. But the great majority of southern slaveholders, including the great proportion of the leaders of the South, never seriously contemplated such a course. Even George Fitzhugh, Eugene Genovese's premier proslavery ideologue, became an agent of the Freedmen's Bureau in Virginia. Some of those

5. David M. Potter, The Impending Crisis, 1848–1861 (New York: Harper and Row, 1976), 469.
6. Henry W. Hilliard, Politics and Pen Pictures at Home and Abroad (New York: G. P. Putnam's Sons, 1892), 421.

who did leave the South right after Appomattox, like Jubal Early and Matthew F. Maury, changed their minds when they found out how American they were. As noted earlier, Kenneth Stampp has been so impressed by the ready acceptance of emancipation in the South as to argue that southerners really did not want to win the war secession brought, that subconsciously they almost hoped to lose because slavery made them feel so guilty or so out of tune with their times. Many southerners, as we know from their writings and their behavior, felt guilty about holding fellow human beings in bondage, but we do not need to go as far as Stampp does in linking these doubts to a lack of commitment to winning the war. After all, no people of modern times, except perhaps those of the Soviet Union in the Second World War have made proportionately such heavy sacrifices of life as the people of the Confederacy. Those sacrifices alone ought to convince us that the War for Southern Independence was not halfheartedly fought. But that conclusion still leaves us with the anomaly of a war to protect slavery that ended with almost a sigh of relief when the peculiar institution was ended.

That anomaly, however, suggests that important as slavery undoubtedly was in shaping the economy and thought of the antebellum South, its presence had not resulted in a novel world view. Southerners relinquished the source of that allegedly different world view much too quickly for slavery to have been firmly integrated into their value structure. Southerners were simply too much a part of the bourgeois world to accept slavery wholeheartedly as someone like Fitzhugh—or Eugene Genovese—thought they ought to.

I do not want to push my interpretation of a smooth transition from a slave society to one without slavery too far or too hard. One must admit that the abolition of slavery marked a significant change in the lives of southerners, white as well as black. Certainly it was a discontinuity in southern history. All questions of continuity are necessarily relative, however; for all history is a combination of varying degrees of continuity and change. The Civil War was certainly a discontinuity in the life of the United States; yet C. Vann Woodward, who emphasizes the deep discontinuities in southern history, contrasts the regional experience with what he calls the smooth flow of American history. To him the Civil War was a minor discontinuity for the North. It is my contention that the end of the Old South did not mark a significant break in the flow of southern history; it was only a minor disruption, with limited effects. This is not to say that the death of slavery went completely unnoticed or even unlamented. Yet it is worth observing that emancipation was not accompanied by the kind of emotional resistance that a challenge to deeply held values can be expected to call forth. The reason I can say this with some confidence is that when deeply held values *were challenged*, southerners did resist with strong emotion and tenacious determination.

What I refer to, of course, is the reaction of white southerners to the impact of Reconstruction after the war. Some years ago, in response to Kenneth Stampp's observation that the end of slavery was abrupt and did not entail what today we would call a "resistance" movement, David Potter pointed out that the Civil War was a war without a resistance whereas Reconstruction was a resistance without a war. What Potter was telling us was that Reconstruction ought to be recognized as a true people's war on the part of the southern whites against the imposition of Negro political equality by northern political and military power. Local control of government and Negro inequality had long been values of southern life, as they were of American life nationally. Slavery had always been not only a system of labor, but a means of controlling blacks as well. One of the South's prime reasons for resisting the end of slavery during four years of war, aside from the pecuniary loss emancipation would bring, was the conviction of most white southerners that blacks would not work with out compulsion. This argument runs all through the public and private writings of planters before and during the war, as James L. Roark's recent researches have abundantly shown. But once slavery was destroyed by the sword, southerners soon found that they could still use free black labor in much the same way and that free blacks could still be socially subordinated to whites. When the northern conquerors began to interfere with the whites' control over blacks, the South reacted violently. For that reason Reconstruction might well be considered a prolonged period of guerrilla warfare on the part of the white South to resist the attempt to interfere with the region's traditional attitudes toward and relationships with black people. To many white southerners—and not without reason—Reconstruction was an attempt to make the South over in the image of the North and, above all, to impose upon the South what the North itself had come to adopt only lately, namely the introduction of black men into political life as voters and officeholders. For it is a fact that until the Fifteenth Amendment was ratified in 1870, more southern than northern states, thanks to the Reconstruction acts, extended the ballot to black men. (Of the twenty states that permitted blacks to vote at that time only seven had done so voluntarily through the ballot box or by popular, democratic means.)

From this perspective, Reconstruction reveals much about the priorities of southern thinking and southern identity. Slavery had won the allegiance of many white southerners, but it was soon discovered that slavery was not indispensable for growing cotton or controlling blacks. What white southerners—even working-class whites—could not abide, so Reconstruction tells us, was the prospect of bringing blacks to the social and political level of whites. Southerners, in short, could accept the end of slavery, but they could not accept the end of white supremacy, especially when it was imposed by a North whose own hands in this respect were far from clean.

Today we no longer portray Reconstruction as the blackout of good government or as the domination of whites by Negroes, in the way that older historians of the South did. But our modern view of Reconstruction, however accurate it may be, does not diminish the way in which popular southern memories and myths of Reconstruction reenforced the differences between the sections and further enhanced the distinctiveness of the South. For years after 1877 southerners would recall those days that followed the war, when the white South had successfully resisted the North and turned back the attempt to impose black power upon a defeated South. Not even in the early years of secession, so the myth would go, had the southern people been so united as when they stood in solid phalanx, regardless of class, against the blacks and their carpetbag allies from the North. Those white southerners who failed to recognize the enduring value of white supremacy at its moment of danger were cast into the outer darkness, to be regarded forever as scalawags, traitors to the South. In time, too, the southern version of Reconstruction became the national version, thus making nationwide the perception of the South as a region distinct in this respect as well as others.

But the undoubted contribution of Reconstruction to southern distinctiveness should not cause us to overlook the continuity between the antebellum years and those after Appomattox. Thomas Alexander has documented what he has called "persistent whiggery" in the Reconstruction years as one measure of the continuance of the old political and partisan rivalries and outlooks across the chasm of Civil War and emancipation. The Whig party was the victim of the drive during the 1850s to create a one-party South in order to defend slavery. But the antagonism between Whig and Democrat did not die, even though old Whigs and old Democrats after the war often called themselves Democrats. For many years after the war ended, the only way Democrats could get touchy former-Whigs to join them was to drop the official and traditional name of their party in favor of the more nonpartisan "Conservative." Clement Eaton in his *Waning of the Old South Civilization* has shown how the practices and values of the Old South continued into Reconstruction and beyond. He compares the South with the late Middle Ages in Jan Huizinga's book from which his title is taken. Just as France and the Netherlands of the fourteenth and fifteenth centuries "remained medieval at heart," Eaton observes, "so did the South in 1880 remain strongly attached to the values and philosophy of the Old South, with the one important exception that relatively few regretted the passing of slavery. Despite the trauma of defeat and the political upheaval of Reconstruction, much of the Old South survived, waning very gradually. The old continued to co-exist with the new until the twentieth century." [7]

The continuity of the Old South into the New has been shown in another way in William Hesseltine's study of the acitivites of some 600 former-Confederate leaders in the years after 1865. Of the 656 leaders who lived long enough to make records, only 71 failed to regain a substantial portion of the prestige and wealth they had enjoyed under the Confederacy and before. Over a third of them became active in politics in one fashion or another; many became lawyers, editors, and

---

7. Clement Eaton, *Waning of the Old South Civilization, 1860–1880's* (Athens: University of Georgia Press, 1968), 171.

farmers, as in the antebellum years. But the occupations that attracted many more in the years after 1865 were banking and industrial management. Only 13 of these leaders had been in banking before the war, but 23 of them entered that field after the end of hostilities. Before the war 16 had been in railroading; after the war 73 were. Mining and industry claimed the attention of 14 of these leaders before 1860, but in the years after Appomattox, the figure was up to 34. In large part, of course, this shift in occupational interest was a reflection of the expansion of industry and railroading in the postwar years. At the same time, however, it suggests that the value structure of the Old South did not preclude a rather quick adjustment to the ending of a slave society. Hesseltine concludes that although many of the Confederate leaders he studied ended the war penniless and often in debt and with families to support, few of them died in poverty. Indeed, many of them became wealthy. The implication is clear: the antebellum South, rather than being a society with a prebourgeois, antiindustrial outlook was sufficiently like the North to have its leaders move quickly from the old into the new order of things. These leaders of the Confederacy did not exemplify the stereotype of the old planter, disheartened and demoralized by his loss of familiar slaves and plantation, sinking into an early and welcome grave on his run-down and depleted acres. Jefferson Davis, as Hesseltine observes, may have found difficulty in adjusting to the postwar order, but Robert E. Lee showed that there was little in the old order that precluded adjustment to, or success in, the new. Lee did not become a railroad executive or an industrialist, but as president of Washington College he showed himself ready to adapt collegiate education to the demands of a commercial and industrial world. As he wrote to a friend who wanted to know in 1866 what he thought about emigrating to Brazil or Mexico, "I

made up my mind on the subject at the first cessation of hostilities, I considered that the South required the presence of
her sons more than that [sic] at any former part of her history,
to sustain and restore her."[8] At no time was Lee's intense
southernism a handicap in the world after Appomattox.

For some years now historians have been writing about
what they refer to as "the New South," so impressed have they
been with the efforts of southern leaders after Reconstruction
to "bring the mills to the cotton." The determined effort to develop the South's industrial resources captured the imagina-
tion of southern boosters long before the historians took it up.
Richard Edmonds and Henry Grady were only the best-known
ideologues of the New South. The very phrase suggests a
sharp rupture in the continuity of southern history. Yet when
we analyze critically the gospel of the New South, continuity
seems more evident than disjunction. As Clement Eaton and
others have noticed, none of the advocates of the so-called
New South repudiated the Old, except for the antebellum
South's reliance upon slavery. Daniel Tompkins, one leading
proponent of a New South, went so far as to conjure up a false
history of the Old South, in which the beginnings of southern
manufacturing in the first two decades of the nineteenth century were said to have been killed off by the proponents of
slavery and cotton growing. In Tompkins' version of history
the development of cotton manufacturing in the South was
not even a new development, but simply a return to an earlier
and sounder South. Richard Edmonds made the same point
when he said in 1903, "The South of today, the South of industrial and railroad activity, is not a new South, but a revival
of the old South, whose broad commercial spirit, crushed by

8. William Tate (ed.), "A Robert E. Lee Letter on Abandoning the South
after the War," *Georgia Historical Quarterly*, XXXVII (September, 1953),
255–56.

the war, is again seen in the development of every line of industry in which this section was bending its energies prior to 1860." [9]

The failure of the New South's Creed to repudiate the antebellum society is not the only sign of continuity. It can also be seen in the persistence of southern patterns of life across the abyss of Civil War, emancipation, and Reconstruction. I say this even though some historians, notably Emory Thomas and Frank Vandiver, contend that the experience of the Confederacy made the South more like the rest of the country. They argue that the very act of fighting the War for Southern Independence, whatever its cause, had the unforeseen and certainly unintended result of making the South into the image of the North, economically and socially. Seeing the Confederacy as a "revolutionary experience," to use Thomas' striking phrase, is a nice exercise in irony, but it does not square with the facts. It is true that the war imposed many changes upon the South, not the least of which was a shift of capital and labor from cotton growing to industrial development, as Eugene Lerner has shown. [10] But these and other changes that Thomas and Vandiver refer to are really temporary consequences of war, not fundamental changes that alter the contours of the society for the future. And the proof of that is the return of the South to the old ways once hostilities had ceased.

The whole economic record of the so-called New South is testimony to the small amount of economic and social change wrought by the Confederate experience. Despite the hopes and propaganda of Henry Watterson, Daniel Tompkins,

9. Richard H. Edmonds, *The Old South and the New* (N.p., n.d., but ascribed to 1903), p. 5.
10. Eugene M. Lerner, "Southern Output and Agricultural Income, 1860–1880," in Ralph Andreano (ed.), *The Economic Impact of the American Civil War* (Cambridge, Mass.: Schenkman Publishers, 1967).

Richard Edmonds, Henry Grady, and countless lesser-known exponents of a New South, by the end of the nineteenth century the South was still an agricultural region with only the rudiments of a diversified and developing economy. Its proportion of manufacturing production in 1900 was smaller than in 1860; the per-capita income of the region was lower in comparison with the North than it had been in 1860. Its proportion of urban population was still the lowest in the nation. In 1850 the South counted one-third of the nation's cities of 25,000 population or more; in 1900 that proportion was down to one-quarter, though its total population was over one-third of the nation's. As J. L. M. Curry wrote his son in 1889, "In choosing the West rather than the South you did wisely, and subsequent history has confirmed the wisdom of the choice—Roseate pictures of the New South are drawn largely by speculators and so far as based on the semblance of truth are applicable to mines and towns—wealth and population seem alike to tend town-ward while agriculture and country languish."[11]

One of the aims of the advocates of the New South had been to attract immigrants to the region, partly to make up for the feared loss of black labor and partly to increase the South's share of skilled workers. Virtually all of the southern states after Appomattox organized commissions or other agencies to foster European immigration, sometimes even sending agents to Europe to entice immigrants to settle in the South. Despite the effort, few immigrants came to the South. In 1910 foreign-born whites constituted 14.5 percent of the population of the United States, but they made up only 2.4 percent of the population of the South Atlantic states and 4 percent of the population in the region comprised of Texas, Oklahoma,

11. J. L. M. Curry to Manly Curry, September 16, 1889, in Curry Papers, Duke University Library.

Louisiana, and Arkansas. Texas, thanks to its border with Mexico, counted the highest proportion of foreign-born in the South: 6.2 percent. At the same time, states far from the Atlantic and Pacific oceans, like Colorado, Idaho, and Wyoming, counted proportions of foreign-born in excess of 12 percent, that is, twice Texas' proportion.

Part of the reason that immigrants did not go to the South after slavery was abolished is that despite the South's stated wish to attract immigrants, the qualifications it set for immigrants were scarcely encouraging. Southern States, the principal periodical devoted to attracting immigrants to the South, made the point clearly enough in 1895, noting that "indiscriminate foreign immigration would be a curse to the South. . . . The South wants and expects to receive a heavy immigration with the next few years; but it must be of the right sort, and she will be found heartily seconding any efforts which may be made to place governmental restrictions on the character of foreign immigrants who seek a foothold on American shores." The journal went on to say that "of the foreigners now living in this country, there are many hundreds of thousands whom the South cannot afford to encourage to settle within her borders." [12] If such was the sentiment of the foremost public advocate of immigration, one can easily imagine the image the South as a whole projected toward Europeans and Asians who contemplated settling in the region.

Philosophical and social objections to certain kinds of immigrants were not the prime reason for the South's failure to attract large numbers of foreign workers. Its relative lack of cities and manufacturing were still at the root of the matter. This is shown quite clearly when one studies the proportion

12. Southern States, III (November, 1895), 401.

of immigrants in the states with large cities and manufacturing. New York's foreign-born population in 1910 constituted almost 30 percent of the whole, and in Illinois the figure reached 44.3 percent. The economic opportunities that were the underlying attractive force for the massive immigration into the United States in the late nineteenth and early twentieth centuries simply did not exist in the predominantly agricultural, rural South. This persistently low proportion of foreign-born, even after the end of slavery, makes plain that it was the lack of economic opportunity in the South—not the immigrants' alleged aversion to slavery—which was principally responsible in the antebellum years for deflecting European immigrants away from the South.

Another measure of the relative lack of economic opportunity in the South is that growth of personal income in the South lagged behind that of the rest of the nation. During the antebellum years, as we have seen, the white South's per-capita income was substantial—not as high as the Northeast's, but better than the Old Northwest's. It was this optimistic prospect that secession and the war presumably interrupted. Or did it? The question arises because when the growth rates for the years 1840 to 1860 are studied it becomes evident that even if the Civil War had not intervened, the South would still have fallen behind the rest of the country economically. According to Stanley Engerman's reworking of Richard Easterlin's basic data, the antebellum growth rates of Mississippi, Alabama, Tennessee, and Kentucky were lower than for the comparably new states of the Middle West. Even without a Civil War to devastate and disrupt the South, these rate differentials—if they had continued—could explain almost alone the South's falling behind the Middle West after 1860. Moreover, as Morton Rothstein has argued, "The records of other plantation areas in modern times must leave many of us unconvinced that, apart from the question of slavery, the commitment to staple commodity production for export could lead anywhere but to disaster." [13] The disaster to which Rothstein refers is not the Civil War, but the widening gap after 1865 between per-capita income in the South and the rest of the nation. The point is that even if one accepts the notion of a prosperous and growing southern economy on the eve of secession, as I do, underneath that immediate success lay the sources for the poverty of the South in the last third of the nineteenth century and after. Thus even if slavery had not been abruptly ended as a result of a devastating war, it is possible to see the origins, if not the fact, of the poverty of the postbellum years in the developments of the prewar decades. Even the South's poverty has a continuity across the divide of war and emancipation.

The physical devastation, the disorganization of production, and the dislocation of labor that war and emancipation brought certainly hastened and deepened the South's economic decline in the years after 1860. By 1880 the per-capita income of southerners was only 51 percent of the national average, though in 1860 it had been 72 percent even when the slaves were counted as income receivers. By 1880 the South lagged far behind the Old Northwest as well, for by then the Middle West had become an industrial as well as an agricultural section of the country. But even the Great Plains area, the prime agricultural sector of the North in 1880 and

13. Stanley Engerman, "The Effects of Slavery upon the Southern Economy: A Review of the Recent Debate," *Explorations in Entrepreneurial History* 2nd Series, IV (Winter, 1967), 87; Morton Rothstein, "The Cotton Frontier of the Antebellum South, A Methodological Battleground," in W. N. Parker (ed.), *The Structure of the Cotton Economy of the Antebellum South* (Washington: Agricultural History Society, 1970), 162.

1900, according to the figures compiled by Richard Easterlin, was far ahead of the South.[14]

The continuity of the South's economy across the gulf of war and emancipation can be observed in more than the continuing dominance of agriculture and the relative poverty of the region. Many years ago Roger Shugg and C. Vann Woodward pointed out that though the census seemed to suggest that the plantations had been broken up by emancipation, in fact they often survived, in substance, if not in the old form. The census-takers counted farms, irrespective of owners, and so the average size of farms in 1880 and after fell sharply from what it had been in 1860. But when a special investigation was made by the Bureau of the Census in 1910, of 325 black-belt counties in the eleven states of the former Confederacy, a different picture emerged. One-third of the landholdings turned out to be organized in "tenant plantations," that is, several tenant farms with a single owner. The average size of these estates held by a single owner with many tenants was 724 acres or, as Woodward writes, "more than six times the average size of holdings reported in 1900 for all holdings."[15] In order to bring the labor of the former slave to the land of the frequently impoverished, though land-rich white owner, southerners developed sharecropping in the years immediately after the war. Under the new regime the gang labor of slavery and the communal slave quarters may have been replaced by individual family tenant homesteads, but the plantation clearly survived in the form of the single white owner of the land directing his many black tenants.

14. Richard A. Easterlin, "Regional Income Trends, 1840–1950," in Seymour Harris (ed.), *American Economic History* (New York: McGraw-Hill, 1961), 528.

15. C. Vann Woodward, *The Origins of the New South, 1877–1913* (Baton Rouge, Louisiana State University Press, 1951), 179.

The persistence of the old ways is shown in more detail in two important recent studies of Alabama by Jonathan Wiener. In a close examination of a single black-belt county, Wiener tested the prevailing view that war and Reconstruction destroyed the old planter class. Using census figures, he shows that not only did the prewar planters hold onto their lands after the war, they actually increased their acreage. Moreover, they successfully resisted the efforts of a new class of merchants to contest their authority over black labor. In fact, the planters assumed the role of merchant as well as of landowner. In a second study of five Alabama counties, Wiener compares the persistent rates of antebellum planters in the postwar years with the persistent rates of other social groups elsewhere in the country. He finds that "the Alabama planter elite is . . . the most persistent rural group known to social science."[16]

The continuity in the organization of agriculture comes through, too, in some of the new studies by economic historians of sharecropping during the late nineteenth century. The central question in these studies is whether cropping was as uneconomical and as exploitative of the farmer as historians have usually believed. Richard Sutch and Roger Ransom, for example, contend that racism distorted the operation of the market system, thus putting the black tenants at an economic as well as a social disadvantage. Sutch and Ransom perceive a high degree of continuity between the slave society of the antebellum years and the so-called free labor society of the postwar decades. The racism inherited from the days before the war continued into subsequent years, thus restricting

16. Jonathan M. Wiener, "Planter-Merchant Conflict in Reconstruction Alabama," *Past and Present*, No. 68 (August, 1975), 73–94; Jonathan M. Wiener, "Planter Persistence and Social Change: Alabama, 1850–1870," *Journal of Interdisciplinary History*, VII (Autumn, 1976), 254.

black expectations and opportunities. White landowners, Sutch and Ransom argue, used race as a "signal" of potential productivity on the part of workers and thus did not deal with black sharecroppers as they would have with white croppers. They simply did not assess black behavior objectively. Ransom and Sutch, by comparing the amount of untilled land on farms among white and black owners and white and black tenants, show that Negroes consistently held less untilled land, a measure that they take as a surrogate of capital. Thus they conclude that blacks received less pay and enjoyed less easy access to the capital market than whites.[17]

The Sutch-Ransom conclusions support the view of most historians of the South, who see racial discrimination and hostility shaping the economic situation of black agricultural workers in the South. Not all modern economic historians, however, go along with that view. Stephen DeCanio and Robert Higgs, working separately, contend that the assertion of an irrational, racist response to economic conditions by white landowners has yet to be proved.[18] Operating on the assumption that economic concerns are central in a market economy, they doubt that a white landowner would deprive himself of income simply because of prejudice against blacks. For as economist Gary Becker has shown, discrimination based on noneconomic criteria exacts a cost from the discriminator as well as from those who are the victims of the discrimination. Higgs's and De Canio's work does not deny the existence of

17. Roger Ransom and Richard Sutch, "Debt Peonage in the Cotton South after the Civil War,"*Journal of Economic History*, XXXII (September, 1972), 641–69. See also their forthcoming book, *One Kind of Freedom: The Economic Consequences of Emancipation*, which will expand the documentation, application, and analysis in several important ways.

18. Robert Higgs, "Race, Tenure, and Resource Allocation in Southern Agriculture, 1910," *Journal of Economic History*, XXXIII (March, 1973), 149–70; Stephen J. DeCanio, *Agriculture in the Postbellum South: The Economics of Production and Supply* (Cambridge, Mass.: MIT Press, 1974).

racism; it merely seeks to account for southern agricultural poverty in the postbellum years in ways other than by reliance on racial prejudice.

In pursuit of this objective, Higgs tries to measure the extent of racial discrimination involved in determining the size of black, as compared with white, farms in 1910. Using the census figures of that year, he finds that the difference in the average size of black and white farms in the cotton districts was fifty-nine acres. That is, Negroes' farms were fifty-nine acres smaller on the average than whites' farms. But if the comparison is made with kind of tenure and improvement on farms held constant, then the disparity drops to twenty acres. The underlying explanation for this drop is that it was the superior wealth of the white farmers that accounted for two-thirds of the difference in size of black and white farms, not racial discrimination. The superior wealth of the whites Higgs attributes to the disadvantages of slavery for blacks; as slaves they could not accumulate capital or buy land. The argument, however, is not compelling, since racial prejudice might account for the lack of capital among blacks as much as slavery. Moreover, Higgs finds that at least one-third of the difference in size of farms between whites and blacks is probably the result of racial prejudice.

DeCanio's effort to show that racial discrimination was not at the bottom of southern agriculture's low per-capita income is less vulnerable than Higgs's. But DeCanio's case is no less indicative of the continuity between the antebellum and postbellum years. DeCanio divides farmers into black and white cotton farmers and black and white noncotton farmers. He then works out the productivity of each of the four groups. His conclusion is that the productivity of white cotton farmers was highest, that of black cotton farmers next, black noncotton farmers third, and at the bottom, white noncotton farmers.

On the face of it, DeCanio's evidence would deny racial discrimination, since white noncotton farmers fare less well than black cotton farmers and black noncotton farmers. DeCanio is particularly interested in this conclusion, for it seems to disprove the widely held view that the inheritance from slavery was a burden upon blacks, that blacks earned less in the postwar South because they carried with them the poor habits, the lack of skills, and economically inhibiting values imposed by slavery.

From my standpoint, DeCanio's evidence would seem to deny continuity between the antebellum and postbellum South. It appears to show that the inheritance from slavery did not affect appreciably the life of blacks or the situation of the South in the years after Appomattox, because some whites did less well than some Negroes in agriculture. If slavery had been as devastating for blacks as is often said, one would not find that some whites were actually, on the average, less productive than blacks.

Yet when DeCanio offers his explanation for this finding, the continuity between antebellum and postbellum South reappears. His explanation is what he calls the location and ownership hypothesis. It asserts that where a group stood on the scale of productivity depended on where that group was located geographically on the soil patterns of the South and whether the group was historically high in land ownership. Thus the whites came out on top of the productivity scale when they held their land from antebellum years; and since it is known that the cotton planters had the best land, these whites kept their superior land after emancipation when it was apportioned among farmers. Cotton-growing black farmers came next on the productivity scale, because as former slaves their farms were located on the next-best land of their former masters, who were now probably their landlords.

Black noncotton farmers stood next because they were few in number in the noncotton-growing regions and so, in comparison with the many whites, tended to occupy better land because they, too, worked the land of their former masters. The land that was left was that occupied by the noncotton-growing whites—the land of least productivity. Obviously there are broad historical and economic assumptions in this explanation, but what is germane to our concern here is that even in this instance, where the intention is to play down the long-range effects of slavery, the continuity between the antebellum and postbellum South is relied upon. For DeCanio's explanation once again shows how the patterns of the antebellum years shaped the patterns of the postbellum years, despite the momentous events that intervened.

The continuity of the southern experience, as exemplified by the persistence of the South's commitment to agriculture after the end of slavery, was reinforced by the New South's insistence that the dominance of the white man must also continue in the postslavery era. For as even Henry Grady had to acknowledge, not everything in the New South was novel. "The supremacy of the white race in the South," Grady insisted, "must be maintained forever, and the domination of the negro race resisted at all points and at all hazards—because the white race is the superior race. This is the declaration of no new truth," he maintained. "It has abided forever in the marrow of our bones—and shall run forever with the blood that feeds Anglo-Saxon hearts." [19]

In truth, the North was no more willing than the South to accord equality to blacks in the years after the Civil War. All regions of the nation after the war, as before, insisted upon the subordination of Negroes, though blacks now voted in the

19. Quoted in Paul M. Gaston, *The New South Creed: A Study in Southern Mythmaking* (New York: Alfred A. Knopf, 1970), 118.

South as well as in the North. The essential measure of southern distinctiveness in these years and therefore the continuity in southern history was not the mere persistence of white supremacy, which was, after all, a national, not merely a southern attitude. The fundamental difference between the sections in regard to race was the institutionalization of white supremacy in the South through legal segregation and disfranchisement.

The adoption of these social and political innovations in the 1890s and the opening years of the twentieth century derived from a complex concatenation of events and circumstances, among which the Populist revolt was notable. But certainly more than merely contributory was the fact that the South was the home of 90 percent of the nation's blacks and that southerners still felt what Hodding Carter has aptly called "the angry scar" of Reconstruction. In the North the small number of blacks raised no comparable threat to social and political control and stirred no memories of black men in political office. The South, like the North, had never been without some form of racial segregation in public places. But after the 1890s separation of the races became the hallmark of the South, being insisted upon in even minor public places like telephone booths and tax assessors' windows. The systematic disfranchisement of blacks—and many whites along with them—also departed from northern as well as southern practices since the war. Even the overthrow in 1877 of the last Reconstruction governments in the southern states had not entailed the removal of most blacks from the voting rolls. In the 1890s the massive disfranchisement of blacks and the pervasive legal separation of the races in the public life of the South set the region apart from the rest of the nation. Just as the antebellum South had been known as the region of Negro slavery, so the postwar South became known as the region of segregation and disfranchisement of blacks. The South after the war, like the antebellum South, was the region in which legal institutions, as well as social and political practices, were extraordinarily hostile toward black people.

Not until well into the twentieth century were the social and economic sources and character of the South's distinctiveness seriously altered. At the time of the First World War the exodus of blacks out of the South began in earnest, creating whole new black ghettoes in the major cities of the North. Yet, today, half a century after the black exodus entered upon its full tide, most blacks still live in the South. According to the census of 1970, in no state of the former Confederacy, except Texas, is the proportion of black population less than 15 percent; in no state outside the South was the figure that high. Indeed, only three northern states counted more than 11.1 percent, the proportion that blacks make up in the national population.

Since 1945 the cities of the South have been the fastest growing in the nation, suggesting that by the end of this century or soon thereafter the South may have closed the gap between its proportion of urban folk and that of the remainder of the country. But as we have seen, that gap still exists, still sets the South apart from the rest of America. In 1973, George Tindall's presidential address before the Southern Historical Association stressed the continuing divergence between southerners and other Americans by referring to southerners as an ethnic minority. And a recent collection of essays by him bears the title, *The Ethnic Southerners*.[20] In short, neither in the realm of social fact nor in the realm of psychological identity has the South ceased to be distinctive, despite the changes of the twentieth century.

20. George Brown Tindall, *The Ethnic Southerners* (Baton Rouge: Louisiana State University Press, 1976).

This long persistence of a distinctive South, with its prom-
ise of enduring for many decades to come, is a challenge to
those of us who seek to interpret the American experience.
Too often in generalizing about Americans, whether under
the rubric of national character or simply under the heading
of seeing Americans as a people different from Europeans or
Asians, the South as a part of America is somehow ignored.
The South usually upsets all our glib generalizations about
what America has been and what it is. How can one talk about
the immigrant experience as fundamental to nineteenth- and
twentieth-century America when so few immigrants settled in
the South in those years? Or how can one generalize about the
rise of industry and the spread of urbanization in the last century without recognizing that these social developments were
not, for the South, nineteenth-century phenomena? For the
South they are only mid–twentieth-century developments.
The South's distinctiveness presents a problem to those who
would talk about national character, for southerners indubitably live in America; but, equally indubitably, they are not
like other Americans. They are more conservative, more
nationalistic, more self-identified, more defensive, and more
romantic than other Americans—or so the polls and subjective studies tell us. Their differences can be measured rather
objectively and precisely, too. Southerners are less rich, less
urban, less diverse demographically and religiously, and
more likely to be black than the rest of Americans.

These differences have such obvious consequences for the
people of the South that no one born in the region—or outside
it—can afford to ignore them. Almost seventy-five years ago
W. E. B. DuBois reminded American Negroes of their two-
ness, of their being both Negroes and Americans. No southerner, so far as I know, has yet seen fit to write about the
two-ness of southerners, though I think someone ought to;

certainly the duality is there. Lewis Killian in his *White Southerners* has suggested it, and Willie Morris has alluded to it. Lyndon Johnson, for one, was certainly oppressed by the disadvantages of it. In his autobiography he tells why he considered not running for the presidency in 1964.

I did not believe, anymore than I ever had, that the nation would unite indefinitely behind any Southerner. One reason the country could not rally behind a Southern president, I was convinced, was that the metropolitan press of the Eastern Seaboard would never permit it. My experience in office had confirmed this reaction. I was not thinking just of the derisive articles about my style, my clothes, my manner, my accent, and my family—although I admit I received enough of that kind of treatment in my first few months as President to last a lifetime. I was also thinking of a more deep-seated and far-reaching attitude—a disdain for the South that seems to be woven into the fabric of Northern experience. This is a subject that deserves a more profound exploration than I can give it here—a subject that has never been sufficiently examined. Perhaps it all stems from the deep-rooted bitterness engendered by civil strife over a hundred years ago, for emotional cliches outlast all others and the Southern cliche is perhaps the most emotional of all. Perhaps some day new understanding will cause this bias to disappear from our national life. I hope so, but it is with us still.[21]

Many other southerners undoubtedly have been hurt by it, too. In his memoirs Harry Truman wrote that if Senator Richard Russell had not been a Georgian he would have been president. One does not have to accept Harry Truman's particular candidate to recognize in a flash the validity of his point. Without the accident of John F. Kennedy's assassination, it seems highly unlikely that Lyndon Johnson would ever have become president. Yet, until the election of Jimmy Carter in 1976, Johnson was the only president elected from the South since Zachary Taylor in 1848.

21. Lyndon B. Johnson, *The Vantage Point: Perspectives of the Presidency, 1963–1969* (New York: Holt, Rinehart and Winston, 1971), 95.

C. Vann Woodward has been so impressed by the special experience of the South that at one time he thought southerners had gained from their past a view of the world that other Americans lacked. In his famous essay "The Irony of Southern History," which appeared in 1953, Woodward contrasted the South's experience with that of the nation. He pointed out that "the South had undergone an experience that it could share with no other part of America—though it is shared by nearly all the peoples of Europe and Asia—the experience of military defeat, occupation, and reconstruction." Because of the fact that, as he said, quoting Arnold Toynbee, "history had happened" to southerners, their history had something to teach the rest of Americans. When that history is understood, Woodward continued, we "should at least have a special awareness of the ironic incongruities between moral purpose and pragmatic result, of the way in which laudable aims of idealists can be perverted to sordid purposes, and of the readiness with which high-minded ideals can be forgotten."[22] That innocence, despite the national myth, is not a fact of our national life.

Yet one has only to read Woodward's essay "A Second Look at the Theme of Irony," published fifteen years later, to recognize the danger of reading too much into the differences between southerners and other Americans. For by then Woodward recognized that growing up in the South did not necessarily have the same effect upon all southerners that contemplating the history of the South had had upon him personally. Being engulfed in the southern past had not automatically invested southerners with that sense of limits and of life's complexities that the knowledge of the South's history had provided Woodward. The war in Vietnam and the

22. C. Vann Woodward, *The Burden of Southern History* (New York: Vintage edition, 1961), 169–70, 189.

unfinished Negro revolution, Woodward observed in 1968, brought home to Americans that whatever they may once have thought, success is not automatic. Then comes his own shock of recognition. "If there were ever a time when Americans might profit from the un-American heritage of the South, it would seem to be the present," he candidly writes.

But if history had caught up with the Americans, it would seem that the irony of history had caught up with the ironist—or gone him one better. For in this fateful hour of opportunity history had ironically placed men of presumably authentic Southern heritage in the supreme seats of national power—a gentleman from Texas in the White House and a gentleman from Georgia in the State Department. And yet from those quarters came few challenges and little appreciable restraint to the pursuit of the national myths of invincibility and innocence. . . . So far as the war and the pursuit of victory were concerned, the people of the South seemed to be as uncompromising as those of any part of the country and more so than many.[23]

F. Garvin Davenport, Jr., in his penetrating book *The Myth of Southern History* put the matter even more sharply. He pointedly observed that those who thought the South offered an alternative to innocence and self-righteousness were sounding "hollow by the time of the presidential campaign of 1968 when the two most prominent Southerners were [George] Wallace and Strom Thurmond."[24]

The South has been an alternative to the rest of the nation, for that is one of the unavoidable consequences of its distinctiveness. But, as we have seen, there are limits to that distinctiveness. Perhaps, as Woodward has argued, southern history ought to have made southerners more aware of the limits of

23. C. Vann Woodward, *The Burden of Southern History* (Rev. ed.; Baton Rouge: Louisiana State University Press, 1968), 230.
24. F. Garvin Davenport, Jr., *The Myth of Southern History: Historical Consciousness in Twentieth-Century Southern Literature* (Nashville: Vanderbilt University Press, 1970), 170.

human action and more tolerant of the need for compromise and adjustment. The trouble is that southerners exhibit these traits no more than other Americans.

Limited though the differences between southerners and other Americans may be, they are worth celebrating, as well as recognizing. Too many modern southerners, it seems to me as an outlander, are prone to minimize or even deny those differences between the South and the nation. Not all of the traits that distinguish the South are admirable, to be sure. Yet what region or society is without its social blemishes? Moreover, the transformation within the South on race relations over the last decade goes a long way toward making up for the region's most glaring deficiency. Today, government reports tell us, there is less public school segregation in the South than in the North, and the election of Jimmy Carter to the presidency by the votes of southern whites and blacks tells a story of change in the South that is only beginning to be appreciated. In a profound sense, the great goal of nineteenth-century southern dissenters and Populists—cooperation between blacks and whites—has finally been achieved. Here, too, the South may well be offering an alternative to the nation. In any event, the South's powerful appeal to its own people—black and white alike—as well as to other Americans, has surely been the alternative it embodies and offers: in its landscape of wooded mountains, red clay hills, harsh sand barrens, lush forest, and watery wastes; in the humid feel of its hot climate; in the sweet, exotic tastes of its foods; in the soft, liquid sound and careless elisions of its speech; in its rurally rooted conservatism and provincialism; in the violence and conformity of its social order; in the human warmth and security of its commitment to family and kin; and, above all, in its enduring sense of personal and regional identity born from a history no other American shares.

These and other traits that help us to begin to define the South's elusive distinctiveness have also an additional meaning. Many of those differences, as we have seen, can be traced back into the history of the region. In the apt metaphor of W. J. Cash, which I quoted in the opening pages of this book, "The South . . . is a tree with many age rings, with its limbs and trunks bent and twisted by all the winds of the years, but with its tap root in the Old South" of slavery and the plantation. In the persistence for more than 150 years of those characteristics that have made the South distinctive lies the reality of the continuity of southern history.

Index

Agriculture, southern: climate and, 11–12, 37, 43, 44, 46, 53, 54, 102, 109; tobacco and, 12, 43, 52; and one-crop emphasis, 16; and protective tariff, 37; statistics on, 43; and small farmers, 47–48; postwar, 124; mentioned, 27
Alden, John: and The First South, 28–29
Alexander, Thomas, 110
Antislavery societies, 32
Ashmore, Harry: and An Epitaph for Dixie, 2
Askew, Reuben, 23

Bailyn, Bernard, 101
Banner, James: on slavery and New Engalnd Federalists, 35
Barney, William L.: on secession, 83
Becker, Gary: on discrimination and economics, 121
Biracial society, southern, 17–18, 45
Birney, James: and abolition, 82
Blackford, Mary Minor, 82
Blassingame, John: and early identification of the South, 27–28
Bonus Bill of 1817, pp. 32–33, 35
Boucher, Jonathan: and identification of the South, 28
Breckinridge, Robert, 82
Brown, Albert Gallatin: and inequality of Negroes, 90–91

Brown, Joseph E., 102
Burke, Edmund, 86, 100

Calhoun, John C.: and slavery, 85; and concurrent majority, 86; and Disquisition on Government, 86; mentioned, 87, 88
Cammett, John: on Antonio Gramsci, 72
Campbell, Randolph: on wealth holdings in Wisconsin and Texas, 69
Capote, Truman, 15
Carlile, John S.: and secession, 83–84
Carter, Hodding: on Reconstruction, 125
Carter, Jimmy: and religious convictions, 23; mentioned, 128, 131
Cash, W. J.: and The Mind of the South, 6; and continuity of southern history, 6–7, 132
Cason, Clarence: and Ninety Degrees in the Shade, 11
Chivalry, cult of, 3
Clan values, 4
Clarke, Blanche, 76
Class. See Hierarchy, southern
Clay, Cassius M.: and emancipation, 78–79; as slaveholder, 82
Clay, Henry: and emancipation of slaves, 78; as slaveholder, 82; on slavery, 89, 94

Climate: and southern distinctiveness, 10, 11
Cobb, Thomas R. R., 91
Coles, Robert: and *Farewell to the South*, 2
Confederate Constitution: and U.S. Constitution, 99–101
Conrad, Alfred: on economics of cotton plantations, 46
Conservatism, southern: and religion, 22, 23, 60; and Samuel Stoffer, 23–24; mentioned, 3, 60, 61–62, 127
Cowley, Malcolm, 15
Crime, southern, 24–25
Curry, J. L. M., 115
Curry, Leonard, 48

Dabbs, James: on southern climate and behavior, 11
Davenport, F. Garvin, Jr.: and *The Myth of Southern History*, 130
Davis, Jefferson, 102, 112
DeBow, J. D. B.: and southern boosterism, 52
DeCanio, Stephen: on racism and market economy, 121–24
Demography, southern: and European stock, 17–19, 46–50, 115–17; and slavery, 45
Donald, David: on defeat of South, 103
DuBois, W. E. B.: on two-ness of American Negroes, 127

Early, Jubal, 107
Easterlin, Richard: and southern growth rates, 117, 119
Eaton, Clement: on southern manufacturing, 50, 54; and *Waning of the Old South Civilization*, 111; on New South, 113
Edmonds, Richard: as ideologue of New South, 113, 115
Education, 32
Egerton, John: and *The Americanization of Dixie: The Southernization of America*, 2

Engerman, Stanley: and *Time on the Cross*, 53, 117
Evolution: and southern religious conservatism, 23

Faulkner, William: and *Intruder in the Dust*, 105; mentioned, 2, 15
Fifteenth Amendment, 109
Fishlow, Albert: on internal waterways of South, 37
Fitzhugh, George: on southern industrial growth, 52; as planter ideologue, 85, 87–89, 94, 106–107; and *Cannibals All!*, 87
Fladeland, Betty: on compensating slaveholders, 42
Flush Times in Alabama and Mississippi, 56
Fogel, Robert: and *Time on the Cross*, 53
Folk society: Potter's comments on, 4
Foner, Eric: and northern view of South, 59, 92
Franklin, John Hope: on personal violence, 24; and southern travel to North, 58; and *The Militant South*, 62
Freehling, William: on tariff controversy, 39

Gallman, Robert: on self-sufficiency of plantations, 48
Gaston, Paul: on W. J. Cash, 6; and discontinuity of southern history, 7
Gaston, William, 82
Georgia Scenes, 56
Genovese, Eugene: on northern and southern world views, 5, 6, 64, 67–68, 84, 106; on discontinuity of southern history, 6, 7, 64; and southern manufacturing, 52; and *The Political Economy of Slavery*, 55; and *The World the Slaveholders Made*, 67; Marxist point of view of, 68, 70–75; and *Roll, Jordon, Roll*, 71–72; on Ulrich B.

Phillips, 71–72; on hegemony, 73–74, 80–81; on southern yeomen, 92–93
Glasgow, Ellen, 15
Golden, Harry: and *North Carolina Israelite*, 19
Grady, Henry: as ideologue of New South, 113, 115; on white supremacy, 124
Gramsci, Antonio: Genovese's study of, 72
Green, Fletcher, 90
Green, George: on banking in Louisiana, 53
Griffin, Richard: on southern textile manufacturing, 51
Grimke, Angelina and Sarah: and abolition, 82
Guns: southern attitudes toward, 25

Hackney, Sheldon: on personal violence, 24
Harris, George W.: and Sut Lovingood, 56
Hartz, Louis: and *The Liberal Tradition in America*, 85; on liberal and conservative thought, 86–87, 100
Hayne, Robert: and southern industrial growth, 52
Hays, Brooks: and *A Southern Moderate Speaks*, 23
Helper, Hinton Rowan: and *The Impending Crisis of the South*, 82–83
Henry, Patrick, 101
Herberg, Will: on southern religions, 19
Hesseltine, William: on postwar Confederate leaders, 111–12
Hierarchy, southern: Potter comments on, 3; discussed, 56–57; and slaveholders' power, 70–71; and advantages to southerners, 82; and Fitzhugh, 94
Higgs, Robert: on racism and market economy, 121–22
Hilliard, Henry, 106

Hilliard, Sam: on self-sufficiency of plantations, 48
Hooper, Johnson: and Simon Suggs, 56
Hundley, Daniel: on southern society, 56–57

Industry, southern: and personal income, 17
Isolationism, American: and southern immigrant homogeneity, 21

Jackson, Andrew: and protective tariff, 38–39
Jefferson, Thomas: on northern and southern characteristics, 29–30; and *Notes on Virginia*, 30; and slavery, 34, 41; and Unitarianism, 60–61; and property, 92
Johnson, Lyndon: on disadvantage of being southern, 128
Johnson, Michael: on secession in Georgia, 83
Jones, Charles: and the South as two peoples, 60

Kazin, Alfred, 19–20
Key, V. O.: and southern distinctiveness, 1
Killian, Lewis: and *White Southerners*, 9, 128
King, Rufus, 41
Ku Klux Klan: and attitudes toward immigrants, 20–21

Lander, Ernest: on slaves and textile mills, 53
Lee, Robert E.: as military commander, 102; and postwar adjustment, 112–13
Lerner, Eugene, 114
Lincoln, Abraham: and slavery, 93, 103; and election, 96; and references to God, 100
Literature, southern: and rurality, 14–15
Litwack, Leon: and *North of Slavery*, 91

Locke, John, 85
Louisiana: banking in, 53; steam power in, 53–54; railroads in, 54
Lowe, Richard: and wealth holdings in Wisconsin and Texas, 69
Lubell, Samuel: and American isolationism, 21

McKitrick, Eric: and two-party systems, 103–104
McWhiney, Grady: and *Southerners and Other Americans*, 4
Madison, James: and southern distinctiveness, 29; and slavery, 30; and protective tariff, 38
Manufacturing: southern compared to northern, 50–56, 101–102; and slavery, 51–52; planter hostility to, 52
Mason, George: and southern distinctiveness, 29
Maury, Matthew F., 107
Meyer, John: on economics of cotton plantations, 46
Missouri crisis of 1819–21, pp. 33, 34, 35, 36, 39, 40–41
Mitchell, Margaret: and *Gone With the Wind*, 56–57
Morris, Willie: and *North Toward Home*, 19–20, 128
Mowry, George: on right-to-work, 17

Nationalism: and the South, 21, 105–106, 127
Nativism: and southern distinctiveness, 1
Negro Seamen's Act, 40

Olsen, Otto, 77
Owsley, Frank: and social mobility, 92; and southern disunity, 102; mentioned, 76

Panic of 1819, p. 33
Parker, William: on southern economy, 51
Paternalism, 56

Pease, Jane: on profligacy of planters, 54–55
Phillips, Ulrich B.: and southern racial attitudes, 18; on slavery, 45; Genovese's criticism of, 71–72; mentioned, 1, 3
Plantations: and climate, 12, 13; and slavery, 27, 43, 44, 46–48, 57; and manufacturing, 51–53; and military preparedness, 62
Poinsett, Joel: and protective tariff, 38–39
Poteat, William Louis: and anti-evolution laws, 23
Potter, David M.: and southern distinctiveness, 3–4, 105; on plantation slavery, 44; on North-South similarities, 94; on Reconstruction, 108
Protective tariff: discussed, 35–38; and Tariff of 1832, pp. 38–39

Racism. *See* Slavery
Ransom, Roger: on racism and market economy, 120–22
Reconstruction, 108–10, 125
Reed, John Shelton: and southern group identification, 9–10; on personal violence in South, 24
Religion, southern: range of, 19, 23, 46; conservative nature of, 22, 61; and social gospel, 23
Roark, James L.: and white control of blacks, 109
Rothstein, Morton: on planters and industry, 17–18, 55
Rubin, Julius: on climate and agriculture, 12
Ruffner, Henry, 82
Rural life, southern: Potter's comments on, 4; and population, 15–18; mentioned, 27, 43
Russell, Richard, 128

Secession: and southern distinctiveness, 1, 99; and centrality of slavery, 42, 106; and division of

slaveholders over, 83; and divided popular support for, 95–97
Sellers, Charles Grier, Jr.: and *The Southerner as American*, 4–5
Shipping routes, 49–50
Shugg, Roger: and southern land distribution, 119
Simkins, Francis B.: and *The Everlasting South*, 3
Slavery: and slave societies, 5, 13, 31, 59, 77; and the plantation, 27, 44–45, 46, 57; identification of South with, 30, 40–41; and 1807 prohibition against importation, 31; and Jefferson, 34; recognized by southerners as central to society, 40–41, 77–81, 106; and southern manufacturing, 51–52; and paternalism, 56; and religion, 61; and law, 63; statistics on, 69–70, 76–77; acceptance of, by nonslaveholders, 81–83, 103; as justified biologically, 89–91
Smith, Adam, 85
Smith, William Loughton: on slavery, 30
Southern States, 116
Stampp, Kenneth M.: and "The Southern Road to Appomattox," 5; on southern manufacturing, 54; on cause of southern defeat, 107; on end of slavery, 108
Starobin, Robert: on slaves in industry, 52–53
States' rights: New England defense of, 32; and strict construction of constitution, 36–39
Stealey, John E.: on slavery and manufacturing, 53
Stephens, Alexander, 102
Stoffer, Samuel: on southern conservatism, 23–24
Sutch, Richard: on racism and market economy, 120–21
Sydnor, Charles: on personal violence, 24, 63; on South as part of national culture, 32–33; on states'

rights, 38; on southern reaction to Rufus King's bill, 41

Taylor, William: and *Cavalier and Yankee*, 57–58
Taylor, Zachary, 128
Thomas, Emory, 114
Thurmond, Strom, 130
Tindall, George: on southerners and other Americans, 126; and *The Ethnic Southerners*, 126
Tompkins, Daniel: as proponent of New South, 113, 114
Tredegar Iron Works, 53
Truman, Harry, 128

Unions, southern, 17
Unitarianism, 61
Urban regions, southern: compared to northern, 14, 126–27; and population, 16, 48–50

Vance, Rupert, 10–11
Vance, Zebulon, 102
Vandiver, Frank, 114
Vesey, Denmark: and slave plot of 1822, p. 40
Violence: and southern distinctiveness, 1, 11; personal, 24–25, 27, 59, 63, 64; and the duel, 63; and lynching, 64

Wallace, George, 130
Watterson, Henry, 114
Weaver, Herbert, 76
Welty, Eudora, 15
White, Maunsel, 56
Wiener, Jonathan: and studies of Alabama, 120
Williams, Tennessee, 15
Williams, T. Harry: on Lee, 102
Wise, Henry, 91
Wolfe, Thomas, 15
Wood, Gordon, 101
Woodward, C. Vann: and "Bulldozer Revolution," 2; and difference in North and South, 5,

84; and discontinuity of southern
history, 6, 7, 64, 108; and southern urbanization, 14; on results of
southern defeat, 105; and southern land distribution, 119; and
"The Irony of Southern History,"
129; and "A Second Look at the
Theme of Irony," 129–30
Wooster, Ralph: on slaveholders,
70, 83
Wright, Gavin: on slaveholders, 69

Young, Stark: and southern distinctiveness, 3

Zinn, Howard: and *Southern Mystique*, 1